False Christ Coming

Coming

DOES ANYBODY CARE?

False Christ Coming

DOES ANYBODY CARE?

WHAT NEW AGE LEADERS
REALLY HAVE IN STORE
FOR AMERICA,
THE CHURCH,
AND THE WORLD

WARREN B. SMITH

MOUNTAIN STREAM PRESS

False Christ Coming: Does Anybody Care?
© 2011 by Warren B. Smith

Mountain Stream Press
P.O. Box 1794
Magalia, CA 95954
www.mountainstreampress.org
warren@mountainstreampress.org

Originally titled *Reinventing Jesus Christ: The New Gospel*, published in 2002 by Conscience Press. Many thanks to Conscience Press for their tireless efforts in the publication of the previous edition of this book.

All Scripture quotations, unless otherwise indicated, are taken from the *King James Version*.

Cover design, with photo by bigstockphoto.com (Kativ, used with permission), by D. Dombrowski (LTP).

To order additional copies of this book, call (800)247-6553. For international orders, call (419)281-1802.

ISBN: 978-0-9763492-2-8 (softbound : alk. paper)

Library of Congress Control Number: 2010941795

Printed in the United States of America

CONTENTS

*For all those who have
the eyes to see
and the ears to hear...*

These things have I
written unto you concerning
them that seduce you.

—1 John 2:26

A Note from the Author

THIS book was originally published as *Reinventing Jesus Christ* in 2002. I began writing the book in August 2001. The book was to be an update on the coming false "Christ." Thus, I watched in amazement as key New Age leaders suddenly appeared on prime-time television providing spiritual commentary after the tragic events of September 11th. Most viewers had no idea that these spiritual "experts" were really New Age leaders and that their seemingly positive comments actually cloaked a deceptive New Age agenda—*a Peace Plan*—that was founded upon cleverly repackaged New Age teachings. These teachings were being hailed as the New Gospel of a New Spirituality.

All over the media after September 11th, with their synchronized sound bites and spiritual analysis, New Age leaders were emphatically declaring that terrorism is not defined by what people *do*, but by what they *think* and *believe*. They argued that terrorism is a spiritual problem that requires a spiritual solution. But their solution—a New Age Peace Plan—was no solution at all. For hidden away within their plan, buried beneath all the "positive" exhortations for "love and peace and oneness" was a "selection process" to eliminate biblical Christianity and all of its followers.

The New Age/New Gospel Peace Plan promises *peace and safety* to those who go along with the plan but ultimately persecution and death to all who oppose it. And while this process has never been discussed on *Oprah*, *Larry King Live*, or *Good Morning America*, it is clearly documented in the writings of New Age leaders.

Their "selection process" is "hidden in plain sight" for all those who have the eyes to see, the ears to hear, and the courage to acknowledge that it is a real plan that is being carried out step by step.

The New Age "Christ" and his New Age movement haven't gone away; they are "moving forward" at breakneck speed. What had only been a theoretical New Age threat prior to September 11th, 2001 is now a very real threat—and it is coming right at the world *and* the church.

In this book, I ask some hard but necessary questions concerning church leadership. Why have most church leaders become so strangely silent about spiritual deception and about the New Age/New Spirituality movement? Why are these same church leaders starting to sound more and more like their New Age counterparts? Are they being seduced by the very teachings they should be exposing and renouncing? Are they unwittingly walking the church into a spiritual trap?

To this day, most Christian leaders continue to ignore or merely give lip service to the spiritual deception that is in our midst. As a result, a false "Christ" with a New Age/New Gospel/New Spirituality has accelerated his move into the church. Sadly, hardly anybody seems to notice or care.

If *False Christ Coming–Does Anybody Care?* is read prayerfully and carefully, readers will be able to better understand the deception behind the New Age Peace Plan of the coming false "Christ." Hopefully, by understanding the deception, the reader will be better equipped to stand fast against it.

Warren B. Smith
November 2010

PREFACE

> Beloved, when I gave all diligence to
> write unto you of the common salvation,
> it was needful for me to write unto you,
> and exhort you that ye should earnestly
> contend for the faith which was once
> delivered unto the saints. —Jude 3

IN 1992, I wrote a book about my experiences in the metaphysical New Age movement. The book was titled *The Light That Was Dark.* I wrote the book because I wanted to warn people about the incredibly deceptive teachings of the New Age. From my own experience, I knew just how powerfully seductive the spirit world was and how appealing its false teachings can be.

At the end of my book, I warned that Christian believers were becoming involved in some of these same teachings and deceptions. Spiritual deception is not just something that happens to unbelievers. The apostle Paul went to great lengths to warn the Corinthians not to be deceived by a "Jesus" that isn't Jesus Christ, the Son of God, a spirit that isn't the Holy Spirit, and a gospel that is not the true biblical Gospel (2 Corinthians 11:4). Throughout the New Testament, believers are continually warned not to be deceived by spiritual teachings and experiences that are not from God. Jesus Christ specifically warned his disciples that spiritual deception would be a sign of the end (Matthew 24:3-5).

Today, it is very sad to see so many believers falling under the influence of the same spirit that influenced me when I was in the New Age. This spirit says that it is a time for "breakthroughs" and for the fulfillment of our "destiny"—that there is something "new" and exciting in the wind. This teaching claims that we are in the midst of a great "transition" that will result in a "paradigm shift," and that through "new revelation" and "personal experience" God is in the process of taking the church to a "new dimension" and to a whole "new level." Many Christian leaders these days are so sure that what they are hearing and experiencing is from God, they are rarely testing the spirits, or even considering the possibility that they are being deceived.

The first century Bereans tested their leaders and tested their teachings as they "searched the scriptures daily" to see "whether those things were so" (Acts 17:11). Apostles, prophets, pastors, and teachers were always subject to God's holy Word. "New revelation" never nullified nor superseded Scripture. The Bereans were not impressed by supernatural power and spiritual experiences that had not been tested by the Word of God. They did not depend on signs and wonders and miracles. They depended on the authority and reliability and trustworthiness of Scripture:

> All scripture is given by inspiration of God, and is profitable for doctrine, for reproof, for correction, for instruction in righteousness. (2 Timothy 3:16)

Paul taught that if he or anyone else preached any other gospel—"new revelation" or otherwise—that person should be completely disregarded (Galatians 1:8). The Bible warns over and over again that we should not allow ourselves to be influenced or intimidated by teachings that originate not from God but from the spirit world and from the hearts of men.

> Now the Spirit speaketh expressly, that in the latter times some shall depart from the faith, giving heed to seducing spirits, and doctrines of devils. (1 Timothy 4:1)

> Howbeit in vain do they worship me, teaching for doctrines the commandments of men. (Mark 7:7)

What had been called New Age is now being presented as New Age/New Gospel/New Spirituality. These "new" teachings are not new at all and have actually been around for centuries in one form or another. Whether it was ancient gnosticism, the occult teachings of Helena Blavatsky (1831-1891) and Alice A. Bailey (1880-1949), or the present day New Age/New Gospel channelings, the bottom line has always been the same—everyone is a "part"of God.

REINVENTING JESUS CHRIST

ACCORDING to the New Age/New Gospel, Christ is not a person. *It is an office.* This New Age Gospel teaches that while Jesus of Nazareth occupied the office during His active ministry, He no longer holds that same position. Today, the office of "Christ" is occupied by someone else. And this "someone else" is presently in the process of establishing contact with humanity. This "Christ" intimates that he is already in the world awaiting mankind's call.

Warning that humanity is in peril and facing possible extinction, this "Christ" explains that his New Age/New Spirituality will unify the world's major religions and bring peace to the world. He has communicated these teachings to his designated teachers, who in turn are now conveying these same teachings to the rest of the world.

This "reinvented" Christ teaches that all humanity is the body of Christ. He, as the "Christ," is the head. This "Christ" states humanity's dilemma is that we have forgotten who we are. We are not "sinners" separate from God. We are all part of the one body of Christ and the one body of God. Salvation does not come by grace from accepting Jesus Christ as the Son of God. Rather it is *achieved*—when we accept ourselves *as* Christ and when we accept ourselves *as* God.

The New Age Gospel teaches that when humanity collectively accepts and experiences itself as being a part of Christ and a part of God, we will not only save ourselves, we will save our world. The

"Christ" of the New Age warns that the hour is late. Peace *must* come. He will help. He has a plan. But everyone must play their part.

With "new revelation," often accompanied by direct personal spiritual experience, people are being taught that because they are a part of God they are actually "at-one" with God and all creation. This New Age/New Spirituality teaches that when people have what is described as their "God within" or "Christ within" supernaturally "activated," they actually experience themselves as a part of the "one body" of God which is all mankind. As these same people unite and join together in remembering and experiencing their "oneness" with God and with each other, they feel they are doing the "work" that is necessary to prepare the way for Christ's return.

THE NEED FOR DISCERNMENT

UNFORTUNATELY, undiscerning Christian leaders have not adequately exposed these New Age teachings and, as a result, the spirit behind the New Age has entered the Church.

The Bible warns us not to be ignorant of our adversary's schemes and devices so that we will not fall prey to his deceptive traps ("Lest Satan should get an advantage of us: for we are not ignorant of his devices" (2 Corinthians 2:11). Scripture also tells us that while "it is a shame" we even have to talk about these things, it is important that we expose them and bring them to the light (Ephesians 5:11-13).

Because of my own involvement with New Age/New Gospel teachings, and in light of the many Scriptures warning us not to be deceived and urging us to expose deception, I will attempt to update believers on the accelerated spiritual deception that has been taking place. Hopefully, by providing a general survey of this deception, believers will be more discerning when—in the form of prophetic "new revelations"—these same teachings try to move into their lives and into their churches.

INTRODUCTION

I marvel that ye are so soon removed from him that called you into the grace of Christ unto another gospel: Which is not another; but there be some that trouble you, and would pervert the gospel of Christ. —Galatians 1:6–7

AN amazing thing is happening across the land. Jesus Christ is being "reinvented" and redefined right in front of our eyes and hardly anyone seems to notice or care. And it is happening with great speed. The "transformational" architects and promoters of a New Age/New Gospel are unabashedly trying to overturn God's holy Word and replace the true Christ–Jesus Christ–with a false "Christ" of Antichrist proportions. And it is happening just as Scripture said it would.

Over the last several decades, while traditional Christian believers have been sleeping, a vastly underrated adversary has made significant gains in the spiritual marketplace. In a gradual series of well-conceived and perfectly-timed moves, this ingenious spiritual being has already introduced himself to the world as "Christ."

And his New Age/New Gospel/New Spirituality is now accepted by millions of well-intentioned people around the world. Through his extraordinary use of the mass media, this "Christ" has presented his New Spirituality through a small but powerful network of key people who enthusiastically proclaim his teachings. Convinced their "Christ" is the true Christ, most of those in the network seem to be unaware of his *real* identity. While the network front line is eagerly mainstreaming his New Age Gospel, this "Christ" has been able to remain in the background, overseeing his Peace Plan to birth a new humanity—a new humanity that will be empowered by his spirit, committed to his teachings, and from which he will one day *emerge*.

THE BIBLE WARNS ABOUT DECEPTION

In the Bible, Jesus teaches that in the latter days a spiritual imposter will arise from the world (Matthew 24:15; Revelation 13:1-8). Jesus warns his followers not to be deceived by the many false prophets and false Christs who will precede and prepare the way for this ultimate deceiver (Matthew 24:24). The Bible warns its readers to test the spirits because there are many false prophets in the world and the spirits behind them are not from God (1 John 4:1). Scripture warns that these very real, deceptive, evil spirits tempt men to forsake the true Gospel of Jesus Christ to follow the false teachings of His adversary (Ephesians 6:10-12; 1 Timothy 4:1). And Scripture describes how an extremely charismatic spiritual leader will one day deceive most of the world into thinking that he is Christ. But while pretending to be Christ, this Antichrist figure will actually oppose Jesus Christ (2 Thessalonians 2:1-9).

> Little children, it is the last time: and as ye have heard that antichrist shall come, even now are there many antichrists; whereby we know that it is the last time.
> —1 John 2:18

CHAPTER ONE

HELEN SCHUCMAN, MARIANNE WILLIAMSON, AND A COURSE IN MIRACLES

And Jesus answered and said unto them, Take heed that no man
deceive you. For many shall come in my name, saying, I am
Christ; and shall deceive many. — Matthew 24:4–5

IN 1965, Columbia University Professor of Medical Psychology, Helen Schucman, heard an "inner voice" saying, "This is a course in miracles. Please take notes."[1] Schucman's initial resistance was overcome when the "inner voice," identifying itself as "Jesus," told her the purpose of the course:

> The world situation is worsening to an alarming degree. People all over the world are being called on to help, and are making their individual contributions as part of an overall prearranged plan. Part of the plan is taking down A Course in Miracles, and I am fulfilling my part in the agreement, as you will fulfill yours. You will be using abilities you developed long ago, and which you are not really ready to use again. Because of the acute emergency, however, the usual slow, evolutionary process is being by-passed in what might best be described as a "celestial speed-up."[2]

Baffled by her assignment, but nevertheless obliging, the skeptical Schucman diligently took dictation from this "inner voice." In the seven and a half years of cumulative dictation that became *A Course in Miracles*, Schucman's "Jesus" presents a whole new way of looking at the world. Using Christian terminology, sophisticated psychology, and convincing authority, Schucman's "Jesus" teaches a completely different gospel than the one found in the Bible. His New Age/New Gospel wholly contradicts the Bible's Gospel of Jesus Christ. Schucman's "inner voice," while claiming to be Jesus, actually opposes everything for which the Bible's Jesus stands.

COURSE TEACHINGS

IN brief, *A Course in Miracles* teaches that all is love. And while the *Course* teaches that the opposite of love is fear, it explains that fear is just an illusion based on wrong thinking. It states that the world we see is merely the projected manifestation of our own illusive, fearful thoughts. As each one of us learns to correct our fearful, wrong thinking, it will change not only how we see the world, but also change the world we see. The purpose of the *Course* is to facilitate this change in perception.

According to the *Course*, love is all there is. And because God is love, God is therefore *in* everyone and everything. It states God is sinless, perfect, and "at one" with all creation and that we, as a part of God, are also sinless and perfect in our "oneness" with Him. It teaches that man's only "sin" is in not remembering his own perfect, sinless, divine nature. The only "devil" is our illusion that we are separate from, and not a part of, God. The *Course* tells its readers that a "sense of separation from God is the only lack you really need correct."[3]

The *Course* also teaches that while "Christ" is in Jesus, so "Christ" is in everyone—and that the "Christ" in everyone is their divine connection with God and with each other. The *Course* further teaches that a "slain Christ has no meaning."[4] It states that wrong thinking has produced the misperception that man is a "sinner" and that he needs an external Christ to save him from his "sins." The *Course* teaches that salvation has nothing to do with Jesus' death on the cross. Salvation comes from what the *Course* calls the "Atonement" ("at-one-ment") process.

This "Atonement," or "atoning," is when each person remembers and affirms and experiences their "oneness" (at-one-ment) with God and creation. The "Atonement" is the *Course's* key to undoing "fear" and dispelling the illusion that man is "separate" from God. The *Course* stresses that the healing of the world is dependent upon each person's fulfilling their Atonement "function" to teach this "oneness" to the world. When everyone comes to understand that "all is love and all is God," then "inner peace" and "world peace" will finally happen. Only "fear" and the illusion of "separation" stand in the way of man's attaining this peace for himself and his world.

POPULARIZING THE *COURSE*

A *Course in Miracles* was published in 1975. In 1979, psychiatrist Gerald Jampolsky's book, *Love Is Letting Go of Fear*, became a powerful testimonial and catalyst for *Course* sales as it helped introduce *Course* principles to the popular self-help market. During the 1980s, the *Course* gained a grassroots following of dedicated believers who were often mysteriously led to the *Course* through unusual, seemingly "meant to be" coincidences and circumstances. It was always assumed that these "meant to be" experiences were divinely inspired. Over time, curiosity and interest in the *Course* grew and it became a cult classic for those in the spiritual "know." Believed to be modern day revelation from the real Jesus, this apparent "gift from God" presented new and seemingly plausible reinterpretations to the teachings of the Bible. Because of the *Course*, spirituality suddenly appeared to make much more sense to many people. Yet, even as word spread, the *Course* still remained relatively unknown to the general public.

MAINSTREAMING "CHRIST"

THAT all changed in 1992 when a little known author named Marianne Williamson and her new book, *A Return to Love: Reflections on the Principles of A Course in Miracles*, were featured on *The Oprah Winfrey Show*. In praising Williamson's book about the *Course*, Oprah told her viewers that she had already purchased a thousand copies of Williamson's book.[5]

After Oprah's enthusiastic endorsement, *A Return to Love* shot to the top of *The New York Times* best-seller list and stayed there for months. The false "Christ" of *A Course in Miracles* was suddenly out of the closet. He and his New Age/New Gospel teachings had just been mainstreamed into millions of American homes. Thanks to Oprah, the false "Christ" of *A Course in Miracles* now had celebrity status. But during the interview that day, Williamson and Oprah failed to mention that the "Jesus" of the *Course* is *not* the same Jesus Christ described in the Bible—and that the teachings of *A Course in Miracles* actually contradict and oppose the teachings of the Bible.

Over the years, Williamson has continued to champion *A Course in Miracles* in the media, through her books, and in her public appearances around the country. Her 1997 book, *Healing the Soul of America*, enabled Williamson and the *Course* to make a subtle transition into the political arena. Hoping to inspire a New Age/New Gospel approach to national and world problems, Williamson, along with best-selling *Conversations with God* author Neale Donald Walsch, co-founded The Global Renaissance Alliance. Many well-known New Age Gospel advocates and *Course* proponents were recruited to serve in the Alliance. In fact, one of the Alliance board members, in much the same manner as Helen Schucman, says she too received "new revelation" from an "inner voice" claiming to be "Christ." Her name is Barbara Marx Hubbard.

A COURSE IN MIRACLES

DIRECT QUOTES FROM THE FALSE "JESUS" OF *A COURSE IN MIRACLES*

GOD

There is no separation of God and His creation. (*Text*, p. 147)

God is All in all in a very literal sense. All being is in Him Who is all Being. You are therefore in Him since your being is His. (*Text*, p. 119)

MAN

The recognition of God is the recognition of yourself. (*Text*, p. 147)

When God created you He made you part of Him. (*Text*, p. 100)

JESUS

Is he [Jesus] the Christ? O yes, along with you. (*Manual*, p. 87)

NAME OF JESUS

The Name of Jesus Christ as such is but a symbol. . . . It is a symbol that is safely used as a replacement for the many names of all the gods to which you pray. (*Manual*, p. 58)

CHRIST

For Christ takes many forms with different names until their oneness can be recognized. (*Manual*, p. 88)

CRUCIFIXION

A slain Christ has no meaning. (*Text*, p. 425)

Do not make the pathetic error of "clinging to the old rugged cross." (*Text*, p. 52)

The journey to the cross should be the last "useless journey." (*Text*, p. 52)

ONENESS

The oneness of the Creator and the creation is your wholeness, your sanity and your limitless power. (*Text*, p. 125)

SEPARATION

The mind can make the belief in separation very real and very fearful, and this belief *is* the "devil." (*Text*, p. 50)

ATONEMENT (AT-ONE-MENT)

This is not a course in philosophical speculation, nor is it concerned with precise

A COURSE IN MIRACLES CONTINUED

terminology. It is concerned only with Atonement, or the correction of perception. (*Manual*, p. 77)

By accepting the Atonement for yourself, you are deciding against the belief that you can be alone, thus dispelling the idea of separation and affirming your true identification with the whole Kingdom as literally part of you. (*Text*, p. 131)

The full awareness of the Atonement, then, is the recognition that *the separation never occurred*. (*Text*, p. 98)

The Atonement is the final lesson he [man] need learn, for it teaches him that, never having sinned, he has no need of salvation. (*Text*, p. 237)

REVELATION
When revelation of your oneness comes, it will be known and fully understood. (*Workbook*, p. 324)

PERSECUTION
You are not persecuted, nor was I. (*Text*, p. 94)

SIN
There is no sin; it has no consequence. (*Workbook*, p. 183)

EVIL
Innocence is wisdom because it is unaware of evil, and evil does not exist. (*Text*, p. 38)

ANTICHRIST
All forms of anti-Christ oppose the Christ. (*Text*, p. 620)

DEVIL
The "devil" is a frightening concept because he seems to be extremely powerful and extremely active. He is perceived as a force in combat with God, battling Him for possession of His creations. The devil deceives by lies, and builds kingdoms in which everything is in direct opposition to God. Yet he attracts men rather than repels them, and they are willing to "sell" him their souls in return for gifts of no real worth. This makes absolutely no sense. (*Text*, pp. 49–50)

MARIANNE WILLIAMSON

DIRECT QUOTES FROM *A RETURN TO LOVE: REFLECTIONS ON THE PRINCIPLES OF A COURSE IN MIRACLES*

ON POPULARITY OF HER BOOK

For that, my deepest thanks to Oprah Winfrey. Her enthusiasm and generosity have given the book, and me, an audience we would never otherwise have had. (p. *ix*)

MAN

To remember that you are part of God, that you are loved and lovable, is not arrogant. It's humble. To think you are anything else is arrogant, because it implies you're something other than a creation of God. (p. 30)

We are holy beings, individual cells in the body of Christ. (p. 32)

We are who God created us to be. We are all one, we are love itself. "Accepting the Christ" is merely a shift in self-perception. (p. 32)

JESUS

Even if he takes another name, even if he takes another face, He is in essence the truth of who we are. Our joined lives form the mystical body of Christ. (p. 296)

Jesus and other enlightened masters are our evolutionary elder brothers. (p. 42)

CHRIST-MIND

The concept of a divine, or "Christ" mind, is the idea that, at our core, we are not just identical, but actually the same being. "There is only one begotten Son" doesn't mean that someone else was it, and we're not. It means we're all it. There's only one of us here. (pp. 30–31)

You and I have the Christ-mind in us as much as Jesus does. (p. 42)

ARMAGEDDON

But we can bypass the scenario of a nuclear Armageddon if we so desire. Most of us have already suffered our own personal Armageddons. There's no need to go through the whole thing again collectively. (p. 82)

MEDITATION

Meditation is time spent with God in silence and quiet listening. It is the time during which the Holy Spirit has a chance to enter into our minds and perform His divine alchemy. (p. 281)

MIRACLE WORKER

To become a miracle worker means to take part in a spiritual underground that's revitalizing the world, participating in a revolution of the world's values at the deepest possible level. That doesn't mean you announce this to anyone. (p. 68)

THE DEVIL

While it's true there isn't an actual devil out there grabbing for our souls, there is a tendency in our minds, which can be amazingly strong, to perceive without love. (p. 34)

JESUS

Just when it seems all hope is lost, when it seems as though evil has triumphed at last, our Saviour appears and takes us in his arms. He has many faces, and one of them is Jesus. He is not an idol, or a crutch. He is our elder brother. He is a gift. (p. 47)

REVOLUTION

It is time for a huge revolution in our understanding of Christic philosophy, and most particularly in our understanding of Jesus. The Christian religion has no monopoly on the Christ, or on Jesus himself. In every generation, we must rediscover truth for ourselves. (p. 46)

CHRIST

"I accept the Christ within" means, "I accept the beauty within me as who I really am. I am not my weakness. I am not my anger. I am not my small-mindedness. I am much, much more. And I am willing to be reminded of who I really am." (p. 33)

THE CROSS

"The journey to the cross should be the last 'useless journey.'" (Williamson quoting *ACIM*, p. 298)

CHAPTER TWO

BARBARA MARX HUBBARD
AND *THE REVELATION*

> For we have not followed cunningly devised fables, when we made
> known unto you the power and coming of our Lord Jesus Christ,
> but were eyewitnesses of his majesty. — 2 Peter 1:16

SELF-described "futurist" and "conscious evolutionist" Barbara Marx Hubbard writes that in 1966 she heard an "inner voice" that came in response to a question she had asked aloud and directed to God—"What is our story? What in our age is comparable to the birth of Christ?" After asking the question she said she fell into a dreamlike state and was given an intense vision of the future.[1]

In the vision, Hubbard saw the earth from a distance. She was made to understand that the earth was a living body and that she was a cell in its body. Feeling her "oneness" with the earth, she experienced its pain and confusion. When her vision abruptly fast-forwarded into the future, she could see the earth and its people were now surrounded by a radiant light. She watched as the whole planet was "aligned" in "a magnetic field of love" and lifted up by the brilliant light. Widespread healings took place as individuals experienced the merging of their own "inner light" with the bright light that was surrounding them. A tremendous "force" emanating from the light sent powerful currents of joyful energy "rippling" through the body of humanity. The world celebrated as all the earth was "born again."

The pain and confusion were gone. Love had prevailed. The "inner voice" told her to spread the message of the vision. It said:

> Our story is a birth. It is the birth of humankind as one body. What Christ and all great beings came to Earth to reveal is true. We are one body, born into this universe. GO TELL THE STORY OF OUR BIRTH. . . Barbara![2]

In 1977 Hubbard began to hear this "inner voice" regularly. At one point she was told:

> Have utter faith in my design. Achieve deep peace. Be prepared for a great force to enter your life to do this work. It cannot enter till you have achieved deep peace. Your reward for peace, which can only be achieved by faith, is contact with the great force and the other forces waiting in the wings.[3]

On Christmas Day in 1979, she had a revelation that the presence in her 1966 vision had been "Christ."[4] Then in February of 1980, at an Episcopalian monastery in Santa Barbara, California, she describes how in the midst of "an electrifying presence of light" her higher self "voice" transformed into the "Christ voice."[5] Over the coming months the "Christ voice" gave her more information and insight about the vision she had in 1966 and more first-hand detail about what will one day be taking place in the world. Hubbard understood that it was her mission to continue telling the story of humanity's "birth."

Since 1966, Hubbard has fulfilled her commission from "Christ" to tell his New Age/New Gospel story. From NASA to the former USSR, from the Georgia State Legislature to the United Nations, she has spoken to thousands of people and hundreds of groups and organizations about the "planetary birth experience" she had been shown in her vision. In the process, she has become a respected "world citizen," known and loved by many for her insights about "God" and "Christ" and the future of humanity.

Hubbard is a co-founding board member of the World Future Society.[6] In 1976 she seriously contemplated a run for the U.S. presidency.[7] In 1984, her name was placed in nomination for Vice-President at the Democratic National Convention in San Francisco.[8] Her speech, based on her "Campaign for a Positive Future," was carried live on C-Span.[9] Today she is on a first name basis with many world leaders and proudly describes herself as part of the "New Order of the Future."[10] At least three of her books were funded by her benefactor, the late Laurance S. Rockefeller, through his Fund for the Enhancement of the Human Spirit. She thanks Rockefeller in her books for his generous support over the years. And she specifically thanks him for his "intuition about the 'Christ of the 21st Century.'"[11]

THE ALTERNATIVE TO ARMAGEDDON

THROUGH the years Hubbard has received voluminous information from her "Christ." In her 1993 book, *The Revelation: Our Crisis Is a Birth* (later renamed *The Revelation: A Message of Hope for the New Millennium*), Hubbard and "Christ" "rewrite" the Bible's Book of Revelation. In *The Revelation*, Hubbard's "Christ" provides specific instructions on how a united humanity, purposefully partnering with God, can literally re-create the future. This "Christ" teaches that the "violent" Armageddon script described in the Bible does not have to happen, that it is only a "possible" future, emphasizing that a more "positive" future can and will manifest when humanity—without exception—openly declares its "oneness" with him and all creation. This positive scenario and the means to attaining it is called "the alternative to Armageddon."[12]

Hubbard's "Christ" describes how planet earth is at an evolutionary crossroads. He states that the world is about to make an evolutionary leap that will take all creation to a new level. Those who awaken to their own divinity, by aligning themselves as one with God and one with each other, will evolve. Those who continue to believe in "fear" and "separation," rather than in "love" and "oneness," will not evolve. Hubbard's "Christ" claims that with his help most of mankind will choose to evolve, calling this evolutionary leap "the Planetary

Birth Experience."[13] He refers to it as the coming time of "Planetary Pentecost."[14] The "birth experience" is a shared event in the future, an "Instant of Co-operation,"[15] when everyone on the planet will be mysteriously changed in "the twinkling of an eye," as humanity is collectively born again into a new creation. Those who evolve will actually become a new species as *Homo sapiens* is collectively transformed into *Homo universalis*, or the "Universal Humanity."[16] The "Universal Humanity" will live together as a community of "natural Christs" in the "New Heaven" on the "New Earth" that is the "New Jerusalem."[17]

THE "SELECTION PROCESS"

BUT Hubbard's "Christ," while describing the "birth experience" and professing his love for all mankind, nevertheless warns that there will be no place in the "New Jerusalem" for those who refuse to see themselves and others as a part of God. He describes, therefore, the necessity of a "selection process" that will select out resistant individuals who "choose" not to evolve. This "selection process" is a "purification" that will be accomplished through "the shock of a fire."[18]

"Christ" states that those who see themselves as "separate" and not "divine" hinder humanity's ability to spiritually evolve. Those who deny their own "divinity" are like "cancer cells" in the body of God.[19] "Christ" warns that a healthy body must have no cancer cells. Cancer cells must be healed or completely removed from the body. He describes the means of removal as the "selection process." The "selection process" results in the deaths of those who refuse to see themselves as a part of God.

After the "selection process," the spirit bodies of the departed individuals will continue to be "purified" in the spirit realm. Hubbard's "Christ" emphasizes that they will not be given another physical body and they will not be able to rejoin humanity until they rid themselves of all "self-centeredness." He defines "self-centeredness" as "the illusion" that one is "separate" from God. The self-centered temptation to see oneself as "separate," and not as a part of God, is "evil" and must be "overcome." He also refers to self-centeredness, or this illusion of separateness, as "Satan."

In this future described by Hubbard's "Christ," anyone who refuses to see themselves and others as "God" and "Christ" will be removed by the "selection process." Those professing Jesus Christ as their Lord and Saviour would be subject to this process, as would traditional Jews, Muslims, and all others who refuse to see themselves as a part of God.

> In this future described by Hubbard's "Christ," anyone who refuses to see themselves and others as "God" and "Christ" will be removed by the "selection process."

THE GLOBAL RENAISSANCE ALLIANCE/PEACE ALLIANCE

BARBARA Marx Hubbard, politically well-connected and extremely influential, is a major figure in the emerging field of New Age/New Gospel/New Spirituality politics. Her "Campaign for a Positive Future" is still going strong. And her formal involvement with Marianne Williamson, Neale Donald Walsch, and other New Age/New Gospel leaders in The Global Renaissance Alliance represents a new kind of spiritual activism that is rapidly developing into a social and political movement. In 2005, The Global Renaissance Alliance transitioned into The Peace Alliance. Hubbard's continued political interests are revealed in an article she wrote in a 2000 book titled *Imagine: What America Could Be in the 21st Century*. In the article, a woman very close to her own description becomes President of the United States after a successful campaign for a "positive future." Her character's campaign embraces the slogan "Resolve to Evolve—The Only Solution is Our Evolution." This president is unique in that she is the lead person in a first time ever team presidency.[20]

Hubbard, through her writings and lifelong spiritual and political lobbying, continues to implement the teachings and principles she received from her "Christ." She is presently dedicated to the process of incorporating these New Age/New Gospel teachings into her own local community of Santa Barbara, California. With high hopes that her Santa Barbara "seed group"[21] will become a working model for other communities around the world, Hubbard will no doubt be looking for opportunities to showcase her project.

The fact that Oprah Winfrey has a home in the Santa Barbara area should definitely increase Hubbard's chances of getting some exposure. In a New Age world that says "there are no coincidences," it is interesting to note that Marianne Williamson, Oprah Winfrey, and Barbara Marx Hubbard all have houses just minutes from each other in the Santa Barbara area. If Oprah does for Hubbard what she did for Williamson, we will all be hearing a lot more about Barbara Marx Hubbard, her Santa Barbara "seed group," and the New Age Gospel plans her "Christ" has for this world.

THE "NEW REVELATION"

DIRECT QUOTES FROM HUBBARD'S "CHRIST"* IN *THE REVELATION*

SIN

My beloved church misunderstood me. It preached the corruptibility of humanity when I came to demonstrate its potential for incorruptibility. It propounded the sinfulness of humanity when I suffered to reveal your godliness and to overcome your guilt by demonstrating that you can totally rise above the death of the body. (p. 231)

PURPOSE OF "NEW REVELATION"

Behold, I am writing anew, through scribes on Earth who are willing to listen to me again with new ears, in the light of the present crises on planet Earth. (p. 265)

You must demonstrate the psychological state of universal consciousness as a new norm. That is the first purpose of your writings. (p. 74)

The second purpose of these writings is to call for the completion of the good news concerning the transformation of the world. (p. 74)

The alternative to Armageddon is open to you. This is why we are writing this text. (p. 264)

RESURRECTION

I did not suffer on the cross and rise again on the third day to show you what I could do, but what you can do. *Yours* is the power. *Yours* is the glory. That is my message to you! (p. 100)

CHRIST

You were born to be me. You were born to be partners with God. (p. 148)

The church is the body of believers who are conscious of being me. (p. 102)

RETURN OF CHRIST

I cannot "return" until enough of you are attracted and linked. (p. 66)

MAN

I did not intend for you to deify me, but to deify yourselves as being at the same stage of evolution as I am. (p. 231)

31

THE "NEW REVELATION" CONTINUED

It is not that you must wait for some master from without. You all have the same master from within. That master is me, your higher self, the Christ within each of you who is, right now, hearing the same voice, seeing the same vision of the future, despite all differences of language and culture. (p. 243)

SATAN

Your triumph over Satan, that is, over the illusion of separation, will be a victory for the universal community. (p. 193)

ALIENS

You should know now that there are no aliens in the universe. They are Sons and Daughters of God at various stages of evolution. Yes, they are different—diverse beyond your present capacity to imagine—but they are not alien. (p. 275)

EVOLUTION

Your unfinished species is ready to evolve. The time has come on Earth for this quantum change to occur in many of you. (p. 65)

You shall be enabled by the process of evolution to transcend your own limits. You cannot do it by human will and desire alone. You are to be empowered by the force that creates the universe. (p. 94)

ISRAEL

Israel is the idea of humanity and God as One. It is the idea of the transformation of this world to a New Earth. It is the idea of the transformation of this body to a new body. It is the idea of the selection of the God-centered from the self-centered. It is the idea of evolution of humanity from Adam of the living soul to Adam of the life-giving Spirit, from *Homo sapiens* to *Homo universalis*. (p. 192)

NEW JERUSALEM

The New Jerusalem is the new city which emerges naturally from a New Heaven and a New Earth. It is the human community as a collectivity of natural Christs. (p. 258)

In the New Jerusalem, humanity and God are one. (p. 286)

*According to Hubbard, these transmissions come from "Christ" and "higher voices."

THE SELECTION PROCESS

DIRECT QUOTES FROM HUBBARD'S "CHRIST" IN *THE REVELATION*

Dearly beloved, I approached the crucifixion far more easily than I approach the selection. The crucifixion was done unto my body. The selection will be done unto yours. (p. 197)

The decisive moment of selection has almost come. The judgment of the quick and the dead is about to be made. The end of this phase of evolution is nearly complete. (p. 189)

By your acts you shall be judged as to whether you can evolve, or must be "cast into the lake of fire," which is the second death. (p. 254)

The "second death" is for those of you who cannot evolve by choice, due to some deeply seated error in your understanding of the nature of reality. (p. 267)

It is to open your mind that you will undergo the second death. (p. 267)

[T]he fundamental regression is self-centeredness, or the illusion that you are separate from God. I "make war" on self-centeredness. It shall surely be overcome. The child must become the adult. Human must become Divine. That is the law. (p. 233)

At the co-creative stage of evolution, one self-centered soul is like a lethal cancer cell in a body: deadly to itself and to the whole. (p. 255)

The surgeon dare leave no cancer in the body when he closes up the wound after a delicate operation. We dare leave no self-centeredness on Earth after the selection process. For when we complete the process of the transformation, all who live on will be empowered to be godlike. (p. 240)

The selection process will exclude all who are exclusive. The selection process assures that only the loving will evolve to the stage of co-creator. (p. 303)

After the selection process, you will be born to the next stage of

THE SELECTION PROCESS CONTINUED

evolution. There will be a New Heaven, a New Earth, a new body and a new consciousness for all who survive. (p. 261)

Your triumph over Satan, that is, over the illusion of separation, will be a victory for the universal community. (p. 193)

If you do not choose to have a new body to co-create with me, you will not have one. You may choose an impersonal future rather than the transpersonal future. The impersonal future is bodiless. You divest yourself of your personal memory and your DNA, and become an undifferentiated aspect of God. (p. 196)

Cynics, disbelievers, those who fear and cannot love: know that the mercy of God almighty is with you now. The second death, for you, is a purification, an erasing of the memory of fear, through the shock of a fire. It will burn out the imprint upon your soul that is blocking you from seeing the glory which shall be revealed in you. (p. 267)

Those who are not sufficiently educated to align with the design, experience God's pu-rification process as long as necessary, until they learn how to know God or the Intention of Creation experientially. They cannot return to the new Earth or the new Heaven, in a self-centered state. (p. 255)

Remember, Satan is either consumed by fire or by love. In the New Jerusalem, there is no illusion of separation. (p. 297)

The end is near. The old play is almost over. Suffice it to say, that if you do not choose to evolve into a wholesome, co-creative human, then you shall not. (p. 195)

The only punishment is your self-exclusion from the joy of new life. The only pity is that you are missing the mark and choosing to die unfulfilled. (p. 195)

There need be no greater punish-ment. There need be no threats. There is only choice. That is the purpose of freedom. Only those who choose to evolve, do. (p. 195)

The stakes are high, dearly beloved. Choose well. (p. 290)

CHAPTER THREE

NEALE DONALD WALSCH AND CONVERSATIONS WITH GOD

For the time will come when they will not endure sound doctrine;
but after their own lusts shall they heap to themselves teachers,
having itching ears; And they shall turn away their ears from the
truth, and shall be turned unto fables. —2 Timothy 4:3-4

IN 1992, Neale Donald Walsch, a disillusioned and distraught former radio talk show host, public relations professional, and longtime metaphysical seeker, sat down one night and wrote God an angry letter.[1] He was amazed when "God" immediately answered his letter by speaking to him through an inner voice. That night, and in subsequent conversations, Walsch wrote down all of the dictated answers to his questions. The dictation continued for several years.[2] Walsch's *Conversations with God: Book 1* was published in 1995 and became the first in a series of bestselling *Conversations with God* books. It seemed that in Walsch "God" had found yet another willing channel for his New Age/New Gospel teachings.

In a style reminiscent of John Denver and George Burns in the movie *Oh, God!*, Walsch and "God" present a more "down home" version of the same New Age Gospel teachings that were conveyed through previous "inner voice" dictations to Helen Schucman and Barbara Marx Hubbard. With Walsch playing the role of devil's advocate, "God" cleverly plays off of Walsch's leading questions and comments. Walsch and "God" come across in these conversations as a couple of "everyday Joe's" who systematically dismantle biblical Christianity with their straight-from-the-source, "spiritually correct" teachings. With the assurance of two foxes now in control of the henhouse, they emphatically assert that the New Gospel is from God and that the "Old Gospel" is not.

Delighted by the fact that they are being taken seriously by millions of readers, "God" and Walsch appear to thoroughly enjoy their process of bringing the public up to spiritual speed. Continuing to build upon the foundation of New Age teachings already introduced through Schucman, Hubbard, and others, "God" and Walsch add some special twists of their own to the New Gospel story. Using Walsch as the straight man, "God" introduces many of his more extreme teachings with smug, authoritative statements such as: "There are no such things as the Ten Commandments,"[3] "So who said Jesus was perfect?,"[4] and "Hitler went to heaven."[5]

GLORIFICATION OF DEATH

WALSCH'S "God" makes a number of other provocative statements about Hitler. The net effect is a minimization of Hitler's actions and an obvious glorification of death. The following are two of "God's" comments about Hitler and death:

> So the first thing you have to understand—as I've already explained to you—is that Hitler didn't *hurt* anyone. In a sense, he didn't *inflict* suffering, he *ended* it.[6]

> I tell you this, at the moment of your death you will realize the greatest freedom, the greatest peace, the greatest joy, and the greatest love you have ever known. Shall we therefore punish Bre'r Fox for throwing Bre'r Rabbit into the briar patch?[7]

Walsch, always the public relations man, anticipates reader incredulity at statements like these by expressing apparent surprise and then asking "God" questions that the skeptical reader would probably ask. But in his process of seeming to challenge "God"—which he does with considerable skill—Walsch actually enables "God" to further expound upon and reinforce the thoughts and ideas of his teachings. Not surprisingly, Walsch always seems to come around to "God's" point of view. Even to some of his more extreme views about death and Adolph Hitler.

In his book titled *Questions and Answers on Conversations with God*, Walsch addresses reader concerns about the comments that "God" makes about Hitler and death. One of Walsch's statements of justification is:

> Yet while the books do state that life is eternal, that death is nothing to fear, and that returning to God is joyful, I do not believe that any reasonable interpretation of the material could fairly portray God as condoning the killing of human beings—or brushing it off as if it were of no importance or consequence.[8]

But Walsch does not address the fact that he and other Global Renaissance Alliance board members recommended Barbara Marx Hubbard's book, *The Revelation*, in which her "Christ" clearly describes a "selection process" that will result in the "second death" of all those who refuse to subscribe to his New Age/New Gospel/New Spirituality.[9]

HUMANITY IS "GOD"

AT one point in their "conversation," Walsch's "God" develops the idea that man is not subject to God because man *is* God. His "God" explains that there are no rules and there is no right nor wrong because man, as God, is his own "rule-maker." Walsch's "God" contends that because God and humanity are one, it is therefore up to humanity to determine what God wants to do. If humanity wants to make up a new set of rules this late in the game, humanity can do that because it was humanity, as God, that devised the original rules in the first place. Everything is relative. Everything is up to the prevailing majority. Therefore, because humanity is God, humanity can create whatever rules and whatever future it wants. For example, "God" tells Walsch:

> All of your life you have been told that God created you. I come now to tell you this: You are creating God.[10]

> *You* are your own rule-maker.[11]

> Think, speak, and act as the *God You Are*.[12]

> Your future is creatable. Create it as you want it.[13]

> Create the grandest version of the greatest vision you ever had about yourselves as a human race.[14]

"Conscious evolution," or the process of mankind consciously exercising its authority as "God" to create its own future, is the title of one of Barbara Marx Hubbard's books. "God" tells Walsch he gave Hubbard the title of the book. Walsch's "God" also takes credit for inspiring *A Course in Miracles*:

> **"God":** This is called *conscious evolution*, and your species has just arrived there.

> **Walsch:** Wow, that's an incredible insight. *That's* why You gave Barbara Marx Hubbard that book! As I said, she actually called it *Conscious Evolution*.

> **"God":** Of course she did. I told her to.[15]

> **"God":** *All attack is a call for help.*

> **Walsch:** I read that in *A Course in Miracles*.

> **"God":** I put it there.[16]

"God" makes it clear to Walsch that his modern-day "revelation" is for all those who have never really understood his teachings about man being God. As he was with Helen Schucman and Barbara Marx Hubbard, "God" is indirectly critical of Bible-believing Christians who insist that sin is real and that man is not God. Walsch's "God" contends that the only real "sin" is for man to see himself as sinful and "separate" from God. His "God" says that the only "devil" or "Satan" is the separatist thinking that differentiates between man and God. Echoing *A Course in Miracles*, Walsch's "God" states that only as humanity sees through the illusion of "separation" and "sin" and affirms its own godliness and oneness with all creation, will the planet be saved from ultimate ruin.

NEW AGE/NEW GOSPEL POLITICS

WALSCH'S "God" warns that in the near future people will have to make a choice between the "old" and "new" gospels. The choice they make will have great bearing on the future of mankind. His "God" declares that humanity, by collectively imagining and envisioning its highest hopes and dreams, can consciously create a positive future. "God" expresses great optimism that this New Age Spirituality will prevail and tells Walsch that humanity is standing on the threshold of a "golden" New Age.

> The twenty-first century will be the time of awakening, of meeting The Creator Within. Many beings will experience Oneness with God and with all of life. This will be the beginning of the golden age of the New Human, of which it has been written; the time of the universal human, which has been eloquently described by those with deep insight among you.

> There are many such people in the world now—teachers and messengers, Masters and visionaries—who are placing this vision before humankind and offering tools with which to create it. These messengers and visionaries are the heralds of a New Age.[17]

Regarding how the New Age will be achieved and ultimately overseen, "God" impresses Walsch with the importance of bringing spirituality into politics and government. He tells Walsch:

> When you agree to spread the word, to carry the message that can change the human heart, you play an important role in changing the human condition.

> This is why all spirituality is ultimately political.[18]

> You cannot *avoid* politicizing your spirituality. Your political viewpoint is your spirituality, *demonstrated.*

> Yet perhaps it is not a matter of politicizing your spirituality, but of spiritualizing your politics.[19]

Walsch's "God" is very specific about how this spiritualization of politics should ultimately manifest itself.

> **"God":** Something will have to be new if you wish your world to change. You must begin to see someone else's interests as your own. This will happen only when you reconstruct your global reality and govern yourselves accordingly.

> **Walsch:** Are you talking about a one-world government?

> **"God":** I am.[20]

"God" exhorts Walsch to carry out his mission to change the world and to bring in a spiritually-based new world order by issuing this charge:

> Go, therefore, and teach ye all nations, spreading far and wide The New Gospel: WE ARE ALL ONE.[21]

And certainly Walsch seems to be doing his part. Responding to his "God's" charge to spread the New Gospel and to help establish sympathy for "a one-world government," Walsch co-founded The Global Renaissance Alliance with Marianne Williamson. He also continues to write books, conduct workshops, and speak to large groups around the country.

CONVERSATIONS WITH "GOD"

DIRECT QUOTES FROM WALSCH'S "GOD"

PURPOSE

And so I have chosen you to be My messenger. You, and many others. For now, during these times immediately ahead, the world will need many trumpets to sound the clarion call. (*CWG Book 1*, p. 144)

The purpose of this book, and of all the books in the trilogy we are creating, is to create readiness—readiness for a new paradigm, a new understanding; a larger view, a grander idea. (*CWG Book 2*, p. 36)

NEW GOSPEL

There is only one message that can change the course of human history forever, end the torture, and bring you back to God. That message is The New Gospel: WE ARE ALL ONE. (*FWG*, p. 373)

GOD

There is only One of Us. You and I are One. (*FWG*, p. 23)

God *is* creation. (*CWG Book 1*, p. 198)

There are a thousand paths to God, and every one gets you there. (*FWG*, p. 357)

CHRIST

Many have been Christed, not just Jesus of Nazareth. You can be Christed, too. (*CWG Book 2*, p. 22)

MAN

You are *already* a God. *You simply do not know it.* (*CWG Book 1*, p. 202)

You are the Creator and the Created. (*CWG Book 3*, p. 350)

You are, quite literally, the Word of God, made flesh. (*FWG*, p. 395)

ATONEMENT/ONENESS

You must realize that "atonement" is *just that*—it is "at-one-ment." It is the awareness that you and all others are One. It is the understanding that you are One with everything—including Me. (*FWG*, p. 92)

CONVERSATIONS WITH "GOD" CONTINUED

The *only* solution is the Ultimate Truth: nothing exists in the universe that is separate from anything else. (*CWG Book 2*, p. 173)

EVOLUTION

And do not stay so "stuck" in your present beliefs and customs that you halt the process of evolution itself. (*CWG Book 3*, p. 89)

This truly is an evolution revolution, for now larger and larger numbers of you are creating consciously the quality of your experience, the direct expression of Who You Really Are, and the rapid manifestation of Who You Choose to Be. (*CWG Book 3*, p. 279)

SIN

In truth, there is no such thing as a "sinner," for no one can be sinned against—least of all Me. (*CWG Book 3*, p. 87)

Quite an interesting concept. How did anyone get you to believe that? (*CWG Book 2*, p. 43)

The act of Adam and Eve was not original sin, but, in truth, first blessing.(*CWG Book 1*, p. 56)

EVIL

Evil is that which you *call* evil. (*CWG Book 1*, p. 61)

ALIENS

Walsch: And You're telling me that beings from outer space are helping us with that?

"God": Indeed. They are among you now, many of them. They have been helping for years. (*CWG Book 2*, p. 239)

The time will come when your consciousness will rise and your fear will subside, and then they will reveal themselves to you. Some of them have already done so—with a handful of people. (*CWG Book 2*, p. 239)

NEW WORLD ORDER

There have been those leaders among you who have been insightful enough and brave enough to propose the beginnings of such a new world order. Your George Bush [Sr.], whom history will judge to be a man of far greater wisdom, vision, compassion, and courage than contemporary society was willing or able to acknowledge, was such a leader. So was Soviet President Mikhail Gorbachev. (*CWG Book 2*, p. 199)

PEACE

You can similarly *end all war tomorrow.* Simply. Easily. All it takes—all it has *ever* taken—is for all of you to agree. (*CWG Book 1*, p. 50)

CHOICE/DECISION

This is the eternal moment, the time of your new deciding. (*FWG*, p. 230)

Yet today is a new day. Now is a new time. And yours is a new choice. It is a choice to create anew your personal relationship with Me. (*FWG*, p. 243)

[Pages 41-44 excerpted from: *Conversations with God* (*Books 1, 2,* and *3*) and *Friendship with God*, N.D. Walsch.]

HITLER AND DEATH

DIRECT QUOTES FROM WALSCH'S "GOD"

HITLER AND EVIL

Walsch: Well, I'm going to have to ask the questions here that I know so many people are thinking and wanting to ask. How could a man like Hitler have gone to heaven? Every religion in the world. . . I would think *every* one, has declared him condemned and sent straight to hell.

"God": First, he could not have gone to hell because hell does not exist. Therefore, there is only one place left to which he *could* have gone. But that begs the question. The real issue is whether Hitler's actions were "wrong." Yet I have said over and over again that there is no "right" or "wrong" in the universe. A thing is not intrinsically right or wrong. A thing simply *is*.

Now your thought that Hitler was a monster is based on the fact that he ordered the killing of millions of people, correct?
Walsch: Obviously, yes.
"God": Yet what if I told you that what you call "death" is *the greatest thing that could happen to anyone*—what then? (*CWG Book 2*, p. 36)

HITLER AND DEATH CONTINUED

I do not love "good" more than I love "bad." *Hitler went to heaven.* (CWG Book 1, p. 61)

The mistakes Hitler made did no harm or damage to those whose deaths he caused. Those souls were released from their earthly bondage, like butterflies emerging from a cocoon. (CWG Book 2, p. 42)

So the first thing you have to understand—as I've already explained to you—is that Hitler didn't *hurt* anyone. In a sense, he didn't *inflict* suffering, he *ended* it. (CWG Book 2, p. 56)

There is no "death." Life goes on forever and ever. Life Is. You simply change form. (CWG Book 2, p. 40)

I tell you this, at the moment of your death you will realize the greatest freedom, the greatest peace, the greatest joy, and the greatest love you have ever known. Shall we therefore punish Bre'r Fox for throwing Bre'r Rabbit into the briar patch? (CWG Book 2, p. 36)

If you are a being who chooses to cut out a cancer within you in order to preserve your larger life form, then you will demonstrate that. (FWG, p. 369)

Every aspect of divinity has co-creative control over its destiny. Therefore, you cannot kill a mosquito against its will. At some level, the mosquito has chosen that. All of the change in the universe occurs with the consent of the universe itself, in its various forms. The universe cannot disagree with itself. That is impossible. (FWG, p. 371)

And so, to your question. Is it okay to swat a mosquito? Trap a mouse? Pull a weed? Slaughter a lamb and eat it? That is for you to decide. *All* is for you to decide. (FWG, p. 388)

For while you will understand that you cannot *end* another's life in any event (all life is eternal), you will not choose to terminate any particular incarnation, nor change any life energy from one form to another, without the most sacred justification. (CWG Book 1, pp. 96-97)

CHAPTER FOUR

BENJAMIN CREME, WAYNE PETERSON, AND MAITREYA

I am come in my Father's
name, and ye receive me not:
if another shall come in his
own name, him ye will receive.

—John 5:43

IN February 1982, Wayne Peterson, a director of the U.S. Government's Fulbright Scholarship Program,[1] was relaxing in his Washington D.C. home looking for something to watch on TV. His interest was piqued when he noticed popular talk show host Merv Griffin holding up a book titled *The Reappearance of the Christ and the Masters of Wisdom*. Peterson, a former Peace Corps volunteer and veteran American diplomat, writes that his first thought was that the book had some "fundamentalist Christian message," but he questioned why Griffin would be "promoting" this religious group on his show. Fascinated, he stayed tuned as Griffin interviewed the book's author, British artist and esotericist Benjamin Creme. Peterson recalls what transpired in the interview:

> During this discussion, Creme said that the one Christians call the Christ had reappeared and was living in a major industrial city in the Western world. This time his name was Maitreya and he was bringing with him a large group of his disciples, highly advanced, spiritual men called the Masters of Wisdom. He said we could expect

to hear more about Maitreya on local and international news programs very soon.

Maitreya's purpose, Creme indicated, was to help us realize our innate divinity through learning to live in right relationship as brothers and sisters of one great family. The first step was to establish sharing as the way to eliminate the poverty and starvation that caused millions around the world to die daily in the midst of plenty. Maitreya was emerging in time to help us save ourselves and the planet, and would make himself known to all in a televised "Day of Declaration" soon to come.[2]

As Peterson listened to Creme and heard about Maitreya, he recalled an incident from childhood. As a little boy in the midst of a life-threatening illness, he believed that he had been visited by "Mary," the mother of Jesus. So powerful was her help and presence that he expressed his desire to depart with her rather than stay in the world. In her successful effort to convince him to stay in the world with his family, Peterson states that she told him the following:

> I am going to tell you a secret that few now know. If you stay with your family, you will see the Christ because he will come to live with the people of the world.[3]

UNIVERSAL NEW AGE CHRIST

CONVINCED that Maitreya was the "Christ" that "Mary" had promised would come, Peterson ordered Creme's book. From his reading, he learned more about the "Christ" and his "highly evolved" disciples, the "Masters of Wisdom." Peterson read how these Masters of Wisdom are supernaturally assisting in the evolution of humanity. From his reading, Peterson came to the conclusion that what we commonly refer to as angels are really "Christ" and these Masters of Wisdom. He read that in the future, as humanity transitions from the "old order" to a New Age, there will be more and more open collaboration between these Masters of Wisdom and world leaders in all fields and disciplines. Reading Creme's book, Peterson felt he was beginning to get the big picture:

> As I read Creme's book, I learned more about the Christ, or World Teacher, whose personal name is Maitreya. He is the one awaited by all the major religions albeit unknown to them. The Christians wait for the return of the Christ, Buddhists for the next Buddha, Muslims for the Imam Mahdi, Hindus for a reincarnation of Krishna, and the Jews for the Messiah. These are all different names for one individual, Maitreya, who is here not as a religious leader but as a teacher for *all* humanity.[4]

Benjamin Creme, in *The Reappearance of the Christ and the Masters of Wisdom*, said:

> In the esoteric tradition, the Christ is not the name of an individual but of an Office in the Hierarchy. The present holder of that Office, the Lord Maitreya, has held it for 2,600 years, and manifested in Palestine through His Disciple, Jesus, by the occult method of overshadowing, the most frequent form used for the manifestation of Avatars. He has never left the world, but for 2,000 years has waited and planned for this immediate future time, training His Disciples, and preparing Himself for the awesome task which awaits Him. He has made it known that this time, He Himself will come.[5]

MEDITATION AND THE MASTER WITHIN

WAYNE Peterson's book, *Extraordinary Times, Extraordinary Beings*, is his first person account of his personal involvement with Creme and Maitreya—what he experienced and what he was told. He writes that, amazingly, within weeks of seeing Creme on *The Merv Griffin Show* and reading his book, Creme actually came to Washington, D.C. Peterson was able to meet with him and other followers of Maitreya and participate in a special "Transmission Meditation." Peterson said that this new form of meditation had been sent to humanity through Creme by one of the Masters of Wisdom. Peterson describes the meditation:

> Called Transmission Meditation, it was a service activity in which energy from the Masters was "stepped down" by the meditators and made available to the world. In the process the meditators' own spiritual development was enhanced manifold. I understood that it was another way to help Maitreya and the Masters emerge as soon as possible.[6]

Peterson reports that he has had several dramatic personal encounters with Maitreya and that he directly experienced Maitreya's extremely powerful spiritual energy. In describing one of those encounters Peterson writes:

> As we stood there with spiritual energy flowing freely, I told Maitreya that, if people could experience this energy, they would discard all their earthly notions of "paradise."[7]

Peterson quotes Maitreya in regards to experiencing "living truth":

> The Master is within you. If you follow the disciplines of life the Teacher teaches you, the Master reveals himself within you. Do not be attached to the human form. The living truth is a matter of experience.[8]

In his over thirty-two years of work with the Peace Corps, the U.S. Diplomatic Service, and as a director of the Fulbright Scholarship Program, Peterson writes that he was able to uniquely observe many of the changes going on in the world. For a while he was unaware of others who had also met with Maitreya. Gradually over time he was able to meet others in positions of responsibility who had met privately with Maitreya and the Masters of Wisdom and were now actively working with them. He writes:

> What I did not initially know was that many of my colleagues in government and diplomatic circles had had similar experiences and had also been contacted by members of a group of extraordinary beings, who might be called the elder brothers of humanity, custodians of the Divine Plan for our evolution. World leaders who are household names have privately confirmed their knowledge of and cooperation with this unfolding plan.[9]

MAITREYA, GORBACHEV, AND MANDELA

PERHAPS one of Peterson's chief revelations is that one of the political figures who openly acknowledges that he is working with Maitreya to bring peace to the world is former Soviet leader Mikhail Gorbachev.

> There was one individual, however, who made it clear he had no problem with the public knowing he had met the Christ. His name was Mikhail Gorbachev. Since he was now out of political power in his country, I assume he felt he had nothing to fear or lose from such a disclosure.

> I was not surprised to learn this about Mr. Gorbachev, since I had heard much earlier of his involvement with Maitreya from a Pentagon official. I had also heard, from people I place much confidence in, that Mrs. Gorbachev had been to India several times to see the Avatar Sai Baba. I find it interesting that the international press never questioned Mr. Gorbachev more about his spiritual beliefs, since both he and his wife became

Christians during his term in office. From the freedom and openness he introduced to the Soviet Union, it appeared obvious to me that he was being influenced by the Christ. Eventually, we will hear more of this story and how the Soviet empire collapsed.

What I appreciate about this story is the sure knowledge that the Masters have already undertaken the task of offering important world leaders a role in the coming global changes and of preparing them for the Day of Declaration. These leaders, who are undoubtedly disciples of the Masters, will be working to promote the goals of the Spiritual Hierarchy.[10]

During a November 9, 2001 television interview in Santa Barbara, California, Peterson mentioned that South African political leader Nelson Mandela is another world figure who is actively working with Maitreya. Again, in the metaphysical world where "there are no coincidences," the Santa Barbara television program *Bridging Heaven & Earth*, on which Peterson appeared, was overseen by a board of directors that included Barbara Marx Hubbard.[11]

THE ROCKEFELLERS

PETERSON writes that many years ago, under some very unique circumstances, he was personally recruited into the Peace Corps by Chase Manhattan Bank President David Rockefeller[12] who talked him into joining and actually pulled some strings in regards to his first assignment. That David Rockefeller helped one of Maitreya's chief spokespersons get his start in governmental service, while brother Laurance S. Rockefeller was encouraging and financially supporting Barbara Marx Hubbard, is yet another interesting "coincidence"— especially in light of Peterson's interview on the Hubbard-related television program.

"BLESSED MOTHER" MARY

PETERSON also writes that there are a number of interesting areas of common ground between Maitreya and the "Blessed Mother" Mary.

> Therefore, what I am hearing in the messages from both Maitreya and the Blessed Mother is that, if we are to place our trust in God completely and become Self-realized souls, we must abandon fear. No half way attempt is useful. One must be completely free of fear to experience God, by whatever name we call Him.[13]

> Many interesting parallels exist between descriptions of Maitreya's Day of Declaration and the messages from the Blessed Mother. Both tell us we can expect a major spiritual event that will shake the world. This event, according to the apparitions of the Blessed Mother, will change humanity. Both say it can be easy or difficult depending upon humanity itself. If we decide to change the way we live, we will enter a great and glorious age with relative ease. If we refuse to change our ways, the transition will be difficult and many will suffer.[14]

Peterson continues to be a special advocate for Maitreya. He anticipates being employed as an ambassador for Maitreya after the World Teacher's "Day of Declaration" when Maitreya finally appears and makes himself known to mankind.[15]

MESSAGES FROM MAITREYA

DIRECT QUOTES FROM MAITREYA AND BENJAMIN CREME

NEW REVELATION

He comes now to release that energy of Will and an entirely new aspect of Divinity will be presented to mankind. This is the New Revelation. We have shown that we are ready because we are beginning to sense ourselves as One. (Creme, *Reappearance*, p. 48)

NEW DISPENSATION

They stand ready today to receive the means of change, the outlines of the New Dispensation for this world. They stand ready to greet the dawn of that New Age which beckons all into divinity. (Maitreya, *Messages*, p. 238)

GOD

Every manifested phenomenon is part of God. And the space between these manifested phenomena is God. So, in a very real sense, there isn't anything else. You are God. I am God. This microphone is God. This table is God. All is God. And because all is God, there is no God. (Creme, *Reappearance*, p. 110)

God also sits in majesty on the Golden Throne, and when you are ready, we shall kneel together at His divine feet. (Maitreya, *Messages*, p. 88)

JESUS

He was, and still is, a Disciple of the Christ and made the great sacrifice of giving up His body for the use of the Christ. By the occult process of overshadowing, the Christ, Maitreya, took over and worked through the body of Jesus from the Baptism onwards. (Creme, *Reappearance*, p. 46)

He is one of the Masters Who will very shortly return to outer work in the world, taking over the Throne of St. Peter, in Rome. He will seek to transform the Christian Churches, in so far as they are flexible enough to respond correctly to the new reality which the return of the Christ and the Masters will create. (Creme, *Reappearance*, p. 46)

The Master Jesus is going to reform the Christian churches. (Creme, *Reappearance*, p. 85)

"THE CHRIST" MAITREYA

The Christ is the Embodiment of the energy we call the Christ Consciousness or Principle, the energy of the Cosmic Christ. It is released into the world for us by Maitreya, the Christ, and to the degree that it manifests in us, we will recognise Him. (Creme, *Reappearance*, pp. 48-49)

My plan and My duty is to reveal to you a new way, a way forward which will permit the divine in man to shine forth. (Maitreya, *Messages*, p. 164)

Share with Me, My friends, in a Great Work—nothing less than the transformation of this world. (Maitreya, *Messages*, p. 142)

My Teaching is, as ever, simple indeed. Men must share or die. (Maitreya, *Messages*, p. 272)

MAN

Within all men sits a God. That God is your true Self. (Maitreya, *Messages*, p. 110)

The process of becoming divine is a simple one, a natural one, open freely to all men. It is the process of releasing that God Who, from the beginning, has dwelt within you. My Promise is this: if you will follow Me into the New Time, I shall release for you your divine nature. (Maitreya, *Messages*, p. 58)

My friends, God is nearer to you than you can imagine. God is yourself. God is within you and all around you. (Maitreya, *Messages*, p. 88)

REAPPEARANCE OR "RETURN" OF "THE CHRIST"

My plan is to reveal Myself stage by stage, and to draw together around Me those enlightened souls through whom I may work. (Maitreya, *Messages*, p. 54)

One day, very soon now, when enough people are responding to His Presence and His energy, the Christ will allow Himself to be discovered. (Creme, *Reappearance*, p. 49)

One day soon, men and women all over the world will gather round their radio and television sets to hear and see the Christ: to see His face, and to hear His words dropping silently into their minds—in their own language. In this way they will know that He is truly the Christ, the World Teacher;

MESSAGES FROM MAITREYA CONTINUED

and in this way too, we will see repeated, only now on a world scale, the happenings of Pentecost; and in celebration of this event Pentecost will become a major festival of the New World Religion. (Creme, *Reappearance*, p. 37)

He comes, not as the Head of the Christian, or any other church, for that matter. It may be that the orthodox Christian leaders will be among the last to recognise the Christ. He is not the one and only Son of God, but the friend and Elder Brother of Humanity. (Creme, *Reappearance*, p. 49)

EVOLUTION/ONENESS
I make all men One. (Maitreya, *Messages*, p. 142)

The reason is the creation of the *one* humanity, the idea of the one humanity. This, above all, is the Plan of the Christ. Mankind itself is beginning to sense itself as One; in this coming time it will be One. It is our next step forward in evolution. (Creme, *Reappearance*, p. 151)

When I make Myself known, I shall express the hope of all man-

kind for a new life, a new start, a readiness to change direction; to see the construction of a New World in which men can live in peace; can live free from fear of themselves or their brothers. (Maitreya, *Messages*, p. 18)

ONE WORLD RELIGION
But eventually a new world religion will be inaugurated which will be a fusion and synthesis of the approach of the East and the approach of the West. The Christ will bring together, not simply Christianity and Buddhism, but the concept of God transcendant—outside of His creation—and also the concept of God immanent in all creation—in man and all creation. (Creme, *Reappearance*, p. 88)

ALIENS
I am pledged to silence on certain work for and with the Space Brothers. (Creme, *Reappearance*, p. 11)

I predict that you will see over the coming months and the next couple of years, a tremendous increase in U.F.O. activity all over the world—it is already beginning to take place—preparatory to the reappearance of

MESSAGES FROM MAITREYA CONTINUED

the Christ and the externalisation of the Hierarchy, which is going on at the same time. (Creme, *Reappearance*, p. 206)

CHOICE/SURVIVAL
A crisis of decision awaits mankind... Take care where you place your feet: on the steps which lead to tomorrow or—oblivion. (Maitreya, *Messages*, pp. 130-131)

My plan is to reveal to men that there exists for them but two paths. One will lead them inexorably to devastation and death. The other, My friends, My dear ones, will lead mankind straight to God. (Maitreya, *Messages*, p. 34)

We are here together, you and I, to ensure that man chooses the correct path, the only Way which can lead him to God. (Maitreya, *Messages*, p. 40)

[Maitreya quotes excerpted from *Messages from Maitreya the Christ*. Creme quotes excerpted from *The Reappearance of the Christ and the Masters of Wisdom*.]

"GOD" OF THIS WORLD: SANAT* KUMARA

THE BIBLE WARNS
In whom the god of this world [Satan] hath blinded the minds of them which believe not, lest the light of the glorious gospel of Christ, who is the image of God, should shine unto them. For we preach not ourselves, but Christ Jesus the Lord; and ourselves your servants for Jesus' sake. (2 Corinthians 4:4-5)

*Sanat happens to be an anagram for Satan.

ALICE BAILEY
(DIRECT QUOTES FROM HER SPIRIT GUIDE)
All the qualities, the love and the purpose of a supreme Entity, referred to in The New Testament as the "Unknown God," are focussed in Sanat Kumara. (*Rays*, p. 367)

[B]ut each ray quality will serve to implement the expression of pure love, which is the essential and—at this time—the primary quality of the Lord of the World, Sanat Kumara. (*Rays*, p. 387)

"GOD" OF THIS WORLD CONTINUED

BENJAMIN CREME
(DIRECT QUOTE FROM HIS SPIRIT GUIDE)

He is our "Father." God is both within us and can be known—you can see God. In this coming age many, many people will see God, as Sanat Kumara. They will come before Sanat Kumara and take the third Initiation. (Even more will come before the Christ and take the first and second Initiations.) When you take the third Initiation you see God, as Sanat Kumara, the Lord of the World. . . . (*Reappearance*, p. 135)

DIRECT QUOTES FROM MAITREYA "THE CHRIST"

My task is to bring you, My friends, before the Father, before the Gilded Throne of the Shining One, there to present you to Him and establish you within Our Ranks. My Prophecy holds: I shall take before the Father all who are ready in this coming time. That is the Task given to Me by Him Whom we together serve. (Maitreya, *Messages*, p. 126)

I am with you as God's Representative, as the Spokesman for that Divine Being Whose dreams we are. I shall take you to Him when you are ready, when you have passed through the Gates twice, and stood shining before Me. (Maitreya, *Messages*, p. 42)

Note: Maitreya, the "Christ," appears to have at least a fourfold function: (1) Help humanity to remember and experience their oneness with God and with each other. (2) Bring peace to the world through his reappearance or "return." (3) Introduce and oversee radically progressive economic, environmental, political, spiritual, and humanitarian projects around the world. (4) Lead mankind to the feet of the "Father," Sanat Kumara, who is described as being the "Lord of the World."

[Excerpted from: *Messages from Maitreya the Christ*; *The Rays and the Initiations*, A.A. Bailey; and *The Reappearance of the Christ and the Masters of Wisdom*, B. Creme.]

CHAPTER FIVE

THE LIGHT THAT WAS DARK

> Take heed there-
> fore that the light
> which is in thee be
> not darkness.
> — Luke 11:35

HELEN Schucman heard an "inner voice" that claimed to be "Jesus." Barbara Marx Hubbard heard an "inner voice" that claimed to be "Christ." Benjamin Creme and Wayne Peterson claim to have met the "Christ," and both report that he is already here on planet earth. Neale Donald Walsch heard an "inner voice" that claimed to be "God." All of these individuals have written down what they experienced and what they were told in their personal encounters. This information has been published, and these "new revelations" are now regarded by many as the new "word of God." As the new "word of God," these new revelations directly challenge the authority and reliability of the Holy Bible, questioning and contradicting almost every major teaching of the "Old Gospel" and presenting a New Gospel to take its place. As this New Gospel reinterprets the teachings of the Bible's Jesus Christ, it actually opposes Him and presents another "Christ" to take His place. This New Gospel is very powerful and very believable to those with no understanding of the true teachings of the Bible.

OUR STORY

AS New Age believers years ago, my wife and I had no reason to doubt any of the "new revelation" that was coming our way. When we were students of A *Course in Miracles* in the early 1980s, it never occurred to us that Helen Schucman had received her spiritual dictation from anyone other than the real Jesus Christ. As members of A *Course in Miracles* study group, we studied what the "Jesus" of the *Course* said and applied his teachings to our lives. Having never read the whole Bible for ourselves, we thought the *Course* was helping us to understand what the Bible was "really" saying. We accepted the *Course's* interpretation of the Bible completely. It had a certain logic and seemed to make sense. We believed we were on the right path. Meaningful "coincidence" that had led us to the *Course*, and the supernatural signs that often accompanied our study appeared to confirm that we were spiritually where we were supposed to be.

But at the height of our involvement with the *Course*, the Lord intervened. He exposed the darkness that was actually behind the deceptive "peace," "love," and "light" of our New Age/New Gospel teachings. By the time it was all over, it was clear to us that all of our New Age beliefs had been founded on half-truths and lies. Shocked and amazed by this discovery, we came to the conclusion that A *Course in Miracles* was *not* from God and that the "Christ" of A *Course in Miracles* was *not* the true Christ. Because we had not previously been aware of the Bible's real teachings, we had not been aware of Jesus' many warnings about spiritual deception. He said in the last days false prophets and false teachers, accompanied by deceptive signs and wonders, would deceive most of the world into following a counterfeit "Christ" who would pretend to be Him.

AMAZING GRACE

BUT by far the most important lesson we learned in the midst of what turned out to be our "crash course" on spiritual deception was that Jesus *really* did die on the cross for all mankind. On that cross, He defeated sin, death, and a real spiritual being named Satan and called the devil. We learned from our trying, and at times harrowing experiences, that we actually *do* need a Saviour, and that it was only through belief in the atoning death of the true Jesus Christ that we are truly saved.

We learned the hard way that the "Old Gospel" really works, while the New Gospel definitely does not. When we learned to call on the name of Jesus Christ and all that His name stands for, we experienced His victory over an evil presence that had not responded to any of our metaphysical New Age teachings—most especially *A Course in Miracles*. Calling on Jesus literally saved our lives.

How We Were Deceived

THE more we studied the Bible for ourselves and reflected on our own particular situation, the more we came to understand the extraordinary deception of which we had been a part—a deception that was hiding behind New Age/New Gospel teachings like *A Course in Miracles*. In the following lengthy passages excerpted directly from my book, *The Light That Was Dark: From the New Age to Amazing Grace*, I describe my initial understanding of just how badly we had been deceived:

"For some time now, my spiritual teachings had convinced me that I was a sinless, guiltless, perfect Son of God and that I was every bit as much a part of the universal Christ as Jesus or Buddha or anyone else. I had been taught that I was a holy part of God, inherently equal to Christ and that I didn't need to be saved, redeemed, or born again. Because evil was only an illusion, there was no evil to be saved from. I had believed that I was responsible for myself and my world and I was the creator of my own reality.

"But as I looked at those 'truths' now, I could see that they were not truths at all. What was being taught—no matter how cleverly expressed—stood in stark opposition to the actual teachings of the Bible. Couched in spiritual platitudes, the *Course* and the New Age, although pretending to be friends of Jesus and the Bible, were really no friends at all. Like Judas, they betrayed Christ in the name of love and with a deceptive kiss.

"Jesus warned about false prophets who would come in sheep's clothing—even in His name. His words were concise and clear:

> Beware of false prophets, which come to you in sheep's clothing, but inwardly they are ravening wolves. (Matthew 7:15)

"They would look not like an enemy but like someone you could trust, and I was now thoroughly convinced that the *Course* was a channeled wolf in sheep's clothing that came not to praise the Bible's Jesus but to bury His teachings forever—if that were possible.

Something very mysterious had happened on that "old rugged cross" that a whole New Age was doing hand-over-head flips to completely avoid.

"In the midst of my study, I started to understand that for a number of years I had been letting my spiritual teachers—most especially the *Course*—tell me who Jesus *really* was and what His teachings *really* meant. I could see that through my own laziness in never reading or studying the Bible for myself, I had swallowed a false gospel—hook, line, and sinker.

"I realized now that, although I was made in the image of God, I was not God or a part of God in any way. God was God, and I was me. I wasn't Christ or a part of Christ, and neither was Buddha or anyone else. Jesus was *the* Christ, and there was no other. And, in spite of what anyone else tried to say, He *had* won an amazing victory on the cross of Calvary—one that Joy and I had learned to call on time after time. It was a victory that was fully described in the Scriptures and that so many of the old hymns proclaimed.

"Something very mysterious had happened on that 'old rugged cross' that a whole New Age was doing hand-over-head flips to completely avoid. It was the 'victory in Jesus' that A *Course in Miracles* was desperately trying to redefine and explain away.

"Finally, after all we had been through, I was starting to see that the heart of the Gospel is not so much that God helps those who help themselves but rather that God helps those who *can't* help themselves. It was not in affirming our strength but in recognizing our weakness that we had finally learned to ask the Lord for help. It was His grace, not our own self-sufficiency that had saved the day.

"Yet even though we had recognized our need to be saved from the evil that was coming at us, we had stubbornly refused to acknowledge Jesus as our personal Lord and Saviour. Clinging tenaciously to our metaphysical identities, we hadn't understood that our faith ultimately had to be in Jesus, not in ourselves, and that Jesus meant it when He said:

> I am the way, the truth, and the life: no man cometh
> unto the Father, but by me. (John 14:6)

"We had put our faith in ourselves as God and not in God as God; by going within we had gone without. We had grossly underestimated our ability to not be deceived, and we had grossly overestimated the wisdom of our metaphysical teachers."[1]

BIBLE WARNS OF SPIRITUAL DECEPTION

As time went on, I reflected on how the reality of a deceptive spirit world was never mentioned in the *Course* or any of our other New Age teachings. The rest of this chapter, taken from *The Light That Was Dark*, describes how we came to see this:

"When we could finally see through the spiritual deception, most of the Scriptures we had been reading clicked into place. It was as if scales had fallen from our eyes, and suddenly the New Testament was flooded with light. Though we had a lot to learn about other aspects of the faith, it was apparent that we were, by virtue of our having been so thoroughly deceived, already well-versed in the Bible's description of deception.

"Several weeks later, after much study, reflection, prayer, and many more talks with Joy, I sat down by the creek one morning, determined to go through the Scriptures . . . laying out in even more detail what they said about *A Course in Miracles* and the other false teachings that had been woven into our lives. I went back and forth through the Scriptures trying to piece together our spiritual story.

"One of the first passages I looked at talked about 'another gospel' and how susceptible we can be to false teachings that try to change the Gospel of Christ:

> I marvel that ye are so soon removed from him that called you into the grace of Christ unto another gospel: Which is not another; but there be some that trouble you, and would pervert the gospel of Christ. (Galatians 1:6–7)

"I also reread the Scripture . . . that talked about 'another Jesus'—how even those who have already accepted the true Jesus and His Holy Spirit could be deceived by a false Christ.

> For if he that cometh preacheth another Jesus, whom we have not preached, or if ye receive another spirit, which ye have not received, or another gospel, which ye have not accepted, ye might well bear with him. (2 Corinthians 11:4)

"Helen Schucman heard an 'inner voice' that said, 'This is a course in miracles. Please take notes.' The voice, which later identified itself as "Jesus," proceeded to dictate a body of material that completely contradicted the real Gospel of Christ and whose oppositional teachings could only be characterized as 'another gospel,' 'another spirit,' and 'another Jesus.' Most of us who had read, studied, and believed in *A Course in Miracles* never knew or took seriously the Bible's explicit warnings about the deceivers who would come in Christ's name and pretend to be Him.

"And most of us never knew the Bible's explicit warnings that false Christs and false prophets would arise in our midst and seduce us with supernatural signs and wonders to make us think their teachings came from God. Those signs and wonders would be so convincing that 'if it were possible' they would fool even the most faithful believers of the real Gospel and the real Christ.

> For there shall arise false Christs, and false prophets, and shall shew great signs and wonders; insomuch that, if it were possible, they shall deceive the very elect. (Matthew 24:24)

"But even if we had been aware of the warnings, who would have ever suspected that these false Christs and prophets would arise within our very selves and within our spiritual friends and teachers? Certainly the 'Jesus' that arose within Helen Schucman and manifested as an audible 'inner voice' was proof to us all that false Christs and false prophets were not always flesh and blood but could also come in the form of lying spirits pretending to be a 'spirit guide,' the 'Holy Spirit,' our 'higher self,' or in Helen's case, 'Jesus.' The lying spirits delivered not only false counsel but also false teachings, such as *A Course in Miracles*.

> Now the Spirit speaketh expressly, that in the latter times some shall depart from the faith, giving heed to seducing spirits, and doctrines of devils. (1 Timothy 4:1)

"Just so there would be no mistake about where the lying spirits came from and how they operated, the Bible spelled it out in even more detail . . .

> For such are false apostles, deceitful workers, transforming themselves into the apostles of Christ. And no marvel; for Satan himself is transformed into an angel of light. Therefore, it is no great thing if his ministers also be transformed as the ministers of righteousness; whose end shall be according to their works. (2 Corinthians 11:13–15)

"An angel of darkness could cleverly disguise himself as an angel of light. His servants could disguise themselves as teachers of Christ or even as Christ Himself. They were deceivers of darkness from the other side—another gospel, another spirit, another Christ—the ultimate deception. We certainly hadn't gone out looking for deception, but in our spiritual ignorance we had walked right into their clever trap.

"The Scriptures had been prophetic as they described in detail the signs and wonders and false prophets and false Christs and lying spirits. Many of us had been so convinced we were on the right path that we never stopped to question . . . any of the . . . voices that seemed to be divinely inspired; and just as Helen Schucman's 'inner voice' went unchallenged, so did our own inner voices and those of our spiritual teachers.

"In fact, the Bible had not only predicted spiritual deception but actually warned us to 'test the spirits' before we listened to them:

> Beloved, believe not every spirit, but try the spirits whether they are of God: because many false prophets are gone out into the world. Hereby know ye the Spirit of God: Every spirit that confesseth that Jesus Christ is come in the flesh is of God: And every spirit that confesseth not that Jesus Christ is come in the flesh is not of God. (1 John 4:1–3)

"The test is a godly 'Halt, who goes there?' to make sure the spirits are really from God. . . . When *strongly* challenged, a deceptive [evil] spirit will deny that Jesus is *the* Christ *and* that He came in the flesh to earth.

"In some mysterious, God-appointed way, deceptive spirits cannot withstand the Bible's test any more than they could remain in our presence when we commanded them to leave in the name of Jesus Christ. God mercifully provided us with this way of discerning what is really happening. In fact, the *Course's* Jesus himself answered the question of whether or not he was the Christ. His answer, 'Oh yes, along with you,' clearly failed the Bible's test.

"Those of us who had believed the *Course's* Jesus—that he was the Christ and we were too—were deceived into thinking that 'the Christ' was something bigger than Jesus or us or anyone else. But in believing the *Course* and my other spiritual teachers, I had unwittingly become the very person the real Jesus warned me to watch out for:

> Take heed that no man deceive you. For many shall come in my name, saying, I am Christ; and shall deceive many. (Matthew 24:4-5)

"From that first psychic reading, I had been deceived. Led down a yellow brick road by pied piper spirits, I had, with the best intentions, landed in a metaphysical New Age where the Christ proclaimed was not the real Christ at all. A well-orchestrated and exquisitely timed series of supernatural synchronistic experiences had convinced me that my involvement in alternative spirituality was 'meant to be.'

"Following the signs and wonders of deceptive spirits, I had jumped through my spiritual hoops with almost flawless precision. With expert strings being pulled by the other side, I had been seduced by a ball of light, an Indian guru on a Big Sur mountaintop, a former Napa Valley farmer who was now channeling 'the Source,' and *A Course in Miracles* that had been sent by 'Jesus.' As Joy and I both had unknowingly plugged into the spirit world, we never realized that most of the voices we were listening to were part of the deception the real Jesus had warned about.[2]

"What we had thought to be spiritual truth had turned out to be nothing more than fiction. What we had believed to be the fiction of the Bible had ironically turned out to be the Gospel truth. The age of deception that had been predicted was already well on its way.

"In listening to our spiritual teachers, we had missed the many warnings that were being shouted to us from the pages of the Bible. We were, in reality, fallen human beings, prone to temptation, and easily overcome by evil. And although there was no way we could ever save ourselves, we could be saved by Jesus Christ—the true Son of God—whom God sent to set us free.

"I knew now that if being 'a sinner' meant falling short and being in need of salvation and redemption, then I was a sinner. And if 'repenting' meant turning away from my sins and my ungodly ways, then I was ready to repent. And if being 'born again' meant being born again from God on high, then I wanted to be born again.

"I knew I had a lot to learn about Jesus and all of His teachings and that being a disciple of His would be the test of my life. But I was grateful that Joy and I had been given a window into the spirit world in what had turned out to be our crash course on the truth of the Bible.

> It was only after our whole world had been turned upside down and inside out that we had found ourselves right side up at the foot of the cross.

"In some strange and wonderful way, Joy and I had backed into the Gospel and into our faith. It was only after our whole world had been turned upside down and inside out that we found ourselves right side up at the foot of the cross."[3]

In the years following our conversion in 1984, as just described in *The Light That Was Dark,* my wife and I have watched as a somewhat underground New Age movement has evolved into the popularly accepted, worldwide spiritual phenomenon that it is today. It has grown at an exponential rate and is now highly organized both spiritually and politically. As previously mentioned, many well-known New Age/ New Gospel/New Spirituality advocates had joined together to form The Global Renaissance Alliance. A New Age movement, that for so long seemed to be lacking a central core, had now "reinvented" itself. Suddenly, many of its leaders formed a single organization that had a board of directors and even a mission statement.

THE GOSPEL OF JESUS CHRIST

SELECTED TEACHINGS FROM THE BIBLE

NAME OF JESUS

Wherefore God also hath highly exalted him, and given him a name which is above every name: That at the name of Jesus every knee should bow, of things in heaven, and things in earth, and things under the earth; And that every tongue should confess that Jesus Christ is Lord, to the glory of God the Father. (Philippians 2:9–11)

Neither is there salvation in any other: for there is none other name [Jesus] under heaven given among men, whereby we must be saved. (Acts 4:12)

GOSPEL OF JESUS CHRIST

For I am not ashamed of the gospel of Christ: for it is the power of God unto salvation to every one that believeth. (Romans 1:16)

But though we, or an angel from heaven, preach any other gospel unto you than that which we have preached unto you, let him be accursed. (Galatians 1:8)

SALVATION

For God so loved the world, that he gave his only begotten Son, that whosoever believeth in him should not perish, but have everlasting life. (John 3:16)

This is a faithful saying, and worthy of all acceptation, that Christ Jesus came into the world to save sinners. (1 Timothy 1:15)

For all have sinned, and come short of the glory of God. (Romans 3:23)

But God commendeth his love toward us, in that, while we were yet sinners, Christ died for us. (Romans 5:8)

That if thou shalt confess with thy mouth the Lord Jesus, and shalt believe in thine heart that God hath raised him from the dead, thou shalt be saved. (Romans 10:9)

For whosoever shall call upon the name of the Lord shall be saved. (Romans 10:13)

THE GOSPEL OF JESUS CHRIST CONTINUED

BIBLE

All scripture is given by inspiration of God, and is profitable for doctrine, for reproof, for correction, for instruction in righteousness: That the man of God may be perfect, thoroughly furnished unto all good works. (2 Timothy 3:16-17)

If ye continue in my word, then are ye my disciples indeed; And ye shall know the truth, and the truth shall make you free. (John 8:31-32)

JESUS

Jesus saith unto him, I am the way, the truth, and the life: no man cometh unto the Father, but by me. (John 14:6)

Jesus said unto her, I am the resurrection, and the life: he that believeth in me, though he were dead, yet shall he live: And whosoever liveth and believeth in me shall never die. (John 11:25)

For there is one God, and one mediator between God and men, the man Christ Jesus; Who gave himself a ransom for all, to be testified in due time. (1 Timothy 2:5-6)

And he is the propitiation for our sins: and not for ours only, but also for the sins of the whole world. (1 John 2:2)

CRUCIFIXION

For the preaching of the cross is to them that perish foolishness; but unto us which are saved it is the power of God. (1 Corinthians 1:18)

[T]hat through death he might destroy him that had the power of death, that is, the devil. (Hebrews 2:14)

HOLY SPIRIT

But the Comforter, which is the Holy Ghost, whom the Father will send in my name, he shall teach you all things, and bring all things to your remembrance, whatsoever I have said unto you. (John 14:26)

MAN

For we preach not ourselves, but Christ Jesus the Lord. (2 Corinthians 4:5)

[F]or every one that exalteth himself shall be abased; and he that humbleth himself shall be exalted. (Luke 18:14)

THE GOSPEL OF JESUS CHRIST CONTINUED

SIN

If we say that we have no sin, we deceive ourselves, and the truth is not in us. (1 John 1:8)

EVIL

For we wrestle not against flesh and blood, but against principalities, against powers, against the rulers of the darkness of this world, against spiritual wickedness in high places. (Ephesians 6:12)

DEVIL

He that committeth sin is of the devil; for the devil sinneth from the beginning. For this purpose the Son of God was manifested, that he might destroy the works of the devil. (1 John 3:8)

ANTICHRIST

Who is a liar but he that denieth that Jesus is the Christ? He is antichrist, that denieth the Father and the Son. (1 John 2:22)

PERSECUTION

Marvel not, my brethren, if the world hate you. (1 John 3:13)

And ye shall be hated of all men for my name's sake. (Luke 21:17)

Yea, and all that will live godly in Christ Jesus shall suffer persecution. (2 Timothy 3:12)

BOOK OF REVELATION

And he said unto me, These sayings are faithful and true: and the Lord God of the holy prophets sent his angel to shew unto his servants the things which must shortly be done. (Revelation 22:6)

For I testify unto every man that heareth the words of the prophecy of this book, If any man shall add unto these things, God shall add unto him the plagues that are written in this book: And if any man shall take away from the words of the book of this prophecy, God shall take away his part out of the book of life, and out of the holy city, and from the things which are written in this book. (Revelation 22:18–19)

Because, even because
they have seduced my
people, saying, Peace;
and there was no peace.
—Ezekiel 13:10

CHAPTER SIX

THE GLOBAL RENAISSANCE ALLIANCE/ PEACE ALLIANCE

Behold, they shall surely gather together, but not by me.

—Isaiah 54:15

MARIANNE Williamson's radical transformation from a little known author appearing on *The Oprah Winfrey Show* in 1992 to best-selling author, "spiritual leader," and co-founder of The Global Renaissance Alliance has been remarkable to say the least. As already noted, Winfrey's enthusiastic public endorsement of Williamson's book, *A Return to Love: Reflections on the Principles of A Course in Miracles*, made Williamson, her book, and the *Course* instantly famous.

While *A Return to Love* made Williamson a key player in the contemporary spiritual arena, a subsequent book, *Healing the Soul of America*, has brought Williamson and her New Age/New Gospel message into the political arena. The combined message of these two books is that we, the people, can heal the soul of America and the soul of the world if we "return to love" by accepting the New Age Gospel along with its *A Course in Miracles*-based principles. Because of the popularity of her books and her continued favored status in the media, Williamson has fast become a key ambassador for the New Age/New Gospel/New Spirituality Christ.

After the tragic events of September 11th, 2001, Williamson became one of the "experts" the media called upon to provide support to the nation and to make suggestions about how we should spiritually respond to these disastrous events. With everyone's heightened concern about terrorism and the general state of the world, Williamson and other New Age activists were introducing spiritual strategies for America's future. Suddenly, "spiritual politics" became center stage as the New Age "Christ" brought his updated spiritual teachings into everyone's living room—whether people knew it or not.

Desirous of establishing a single, unified organization to help create peace, Marianne Williamson joined with *Conversations with God* author Neale Donald Walsch to co-found The Global Renaissance Alliance. Alliance members included a veritable "who's who" of best-selling New Age authors and powerful New Age/New Gospel advocates such as Barbara Marx Hubbard, Gary Zukav, James Redfield, Deepak Chopra, Wayne Dyer, and many others.

The Global Renaissance Alliance became The Peace Alliance in 2005 and describes itself as a "citizen-based network of spiritual activists" whose "mission is to make a stand in our local and national communities for the role of spiritual principle in solving the problems of the world."[1] The unspecified "spiritual principle" is the New Age notion that we are all "one" because we are all a part of "God."

Although the organization presented itself as an alternative to "politics as usual," its members seemed to maintain the old political practice of not being very out front about their real agenda. As expressed between the lines of their writings, one of the obvious goals of the New Age Spirituality and of the Alliance organization was to completely "reinvent" (if it were possible) the traditional Gospel of Jesus Christ. While members taught that all paths lead to God, they knew that there was no place in their new spiritual world order for those who insisted that Jesus Christ was their Lord and Saviour.

The Alliance presented itself as a "grassroots" organization of everyday folks, but it is important to remember that the Alliance was spearheaded by a high level group of New Age/New Gospel advocates who appeared to be operating from a general blueprint channeled from the spirit world years ago by esotericist and occultist, Alice Bailey, who is the author of many channeled works. Her blueprint is continually being affirmed and updated by the more recent "new revelations" received by Schucman, Hubbard, Walsch, Creme, and others. Williamson as much as admits the occultic foundation of the New Age Gospel movement by using words that are the title of an Alice Bailey book, *The Destiny of the Nations*. She also borrows a term frequently used by Maitreya when she describes the "Great Work" of which she is a part. In a revealing passage in her book, *Healing the Soul of America*, Williamson writes:

> Beyond the appearances of history, there is a great and glorious unfolding plan for the destiny of nations. According to the mystical traditions, God carries this plan within His mind, seeking always, in every way, channels for its furtherance. His plan for the evolution of humanity, and the preparation of teachers to guide it, is called within the esoteric traditions the Great Work.[2]

The significance of Williamson, Walsch, Hubbard, and other influential New Age leaders choosing to demonstrate their unity and oneness through their global association cannot be overstated. The amount of networking and mutual support among Alliance members is widespread as they continue to join together in increasingly powerful ways to put their New Age/New Spirituality agenda before an anxious world that is searching for spiritual answers. Furthering their common cause, Walsch wrote the introduction to Hubbard's last two books, *Conscious Evolution* and *Emergence*. Hubbard, in turn, recommends Walsch's and Williamson's books in her writings. Williamson does the same with Walsch and Hubbard. The three of them, in their mutual support of each other, provide a strong nucleus for the Alliance's high-powered network of New Age leaders, many of whom have best-sellers and followings of their own.

The Alliance has definitely unified New Age leadership. However, it wasn't until after the events of September 11th that they stepped forward in an even more significant and public way to begin introducing their New Age plan for the conscious creation of world peace.

HEALING THE SOUL OF AMERICA

DIRECT QUOTES FROM AUTHOR MARIANNE WILLIAMSON

There are new ideas on the world's horizon, as different from the twentieth-century worldview as the twentieth century was different from the nineteenth century. (p. 13)

A nonviolent political dynamic is once again emerging, and it is a beacon of light at the dawn of the twenty-first century. (p. 13)

There is a new possibility in the air today, a miraculous awakening and a change in the way we live our lives. It is a spiritual renaissance with social and political implications. (p. 34)

The spiritual renaissance of our time is like a mystical revolution of human consciousness, a surge of energy from the subconscious of a species that registers threat yet is intent upon survival. (p. 40)

Yes, we see there are problems in the world. But we believe in a universal force that, when activated by the human heart, has the power to make all things right. (p. 13)

We need to *declare* peace now, with as much serious effort and intention as that with which a nation declares war. (p. 141)

The bridge to a better world is a shift in mass consciousness. (p. 42)

When a particular group or structure fails to keep faith with the spirit of love—not measured by its words but by its actions—that structure then loses the privilege of guardianship of the great Work. The plan passes on to other groups or structures. (p. 196)

We can change, we will change—in fact, we are changing. That is our destiny. . . . This moment is one of opportunity for the creation of a new civic forcefield. It is up to each and every one of us to decide where America goes now. (p. 197)

HEALING THE SOUL OF AMERICA CONTINUED

The question before us is: how do people who have reclaimed their spirituality best effect political change? (p. 199)

And we expand our perception of spiritual practice to include political activism, that we might most profoundly extend our compassion into the world. (p. 204)

One of the ways to reconnect our personal and political energy is through a project called Citizen Circles. These are small, grassroots groups held all around the country, in which two or more join together to hold the vision of a healed America. (p. 205)

The Citizen Circle is a similar phenomenon, creating a mystical grid of new political possibility around the United States and the world. They help to ground the new political energy. (p. 207)

So it is that a new politics centers around the arousal of that power, using prayer and meditation to create a forcefield of transformation. (p. 209)

A new politics is emerging for the twenty-first century, defining power not by dominance but by sharing. (p. 223)

It is a mystical revolution that will usher in a mystical age. (p. 254)

As a loving critical mass coalesces, as hearts around the world continue to yearn and work for peace, then new forms will emerge to actualize our new planetary vision. This new wine, however, cannot be put in old bottles. The old bottles are inadequate to the task at hand. (p. 255)

ALICE BAILEY (1880-1949)

CHANNELED TEACHINGS FROM BAILEY'S "SPIRIT GUIDE"

NEW GOSPEL

[T]he Christian faith also has served its purpose; its Founder seeks to bring a new Gospel and a new message that will enlighten all men everywhere. (*Rays*, p. 754)

NEW AGE

The New Age is upon us and we are witnessing the birth pangs of the new culture and the new civilization. This is now in progress. That which is old and undesireable must go and of these undesireable things, hatred and the spirit of separation must be the first to go. (*Externalisation*, p. 62)

GOD

All the qualities, the love and the purpose of a supreme Entity, referred to in The New Testament as the "Unknown God," are focussed in Sanat Kumara. (*Rays*, p. 367)

[B]ut each ray quality will serve to implement the expression of pure love, which is the essential and—at this time—the primary quality of the Lord of the World, Sanat Kumara. (*Rays*, p. 387)

CHRIST

Humanity in all lands today awaits the Coming One—no matter by what name they may call Him. The Christ is sensed as on His way. (*Reappearance*, p. 188)

His third activity is the effort to offset the growing hate in the world, to strengthen the trend towards unity, and to show people everywhere the danger of separateness. (*Externalisation*, p. 436)

MAN

This is the challenge which today confronts the Christian Church. The need is for vision, wisdom, and that wide tolerance which will see divinity on every hand and recognize the Christ in every human being. (*Bethlehem*, p. 273)

NEW WORLD RELIGION

The spirit has gone out of the old faiths and the true spiritual light is transferring itself into a new form which will manifest

ALICE BAILEY CONTINUED

on earth eventually as the new world religion. (*Rays*, p. 754)

Workers in the field of religion will formulate the universal platform of the new world religion. . . . This group is . . . a channel for the activities of the Christ, the world Teacher. The platform of the new world religion will be built by many groups, working under the inspiration of the Christ. (*Reappearance*, pp. 158–159)

This inherent fanaticism (found ever in reactionary groups) will fight against the appearance of the coming world religion and the spread of esotericism. (*Externalisation*, p. 453)

PEACE
So peace will come again on earth, but a peace unlike aught known before. (*Rays*, p. 95)

EXPERIENCE
Therefore, in the new world order, spirituality will supercede theology; living experience will take the place of theological acceptances. (*Externalisation*, p. 202)

SEPARATION
Hate and separation must cease. (*Externalisation*, p. 246)

[T]he expressed aims and efforts of the United Nations will be eventually brought to fruition and a new church of God, gathered out of all religions and spiritual groups, will unitedly bring to an end the great heresy of separateness. (*Destiny*, p. 152)

EVOLUTION
Emphasis should be laid on the evolution of humanity with peculiar attention to its goal, perfection. (*Externalisation*, p. 588)

PURIFICATION
It involves the elimination of all that hinders the nature of divinity from full expression. (*Rays*, p. 84)

[Excerpted from the following books by A.A. Bailey: *From Bethlehem to Calvary*, *The Destiny of the Nations*, *The Externalization of the Hierarchy*, *The Rays and The Initiations*, and *The Reappearance of the Christ*.]

And many false prophets shall
rise, and shall deceive many.

—Matthew 24:11

CHAPTER SEVEN

THE NEW AGE CAMPAIGN FOR PEACE

As soon as you—all who know your potentials—can tell this vision
on television, you will have begun your real work in the world.
—Barbara Marx Hubbard's "Christ"[1]

AFTER the terrorist attacks on September 11th, 2001, several key
New Age leaders from The Global Renaissance Alliance suddenly
appeared on network shows that were directly related to the tragic
events. Marianne Williamson was interviewed by Tom Brokaw on
NBC, by Oprah Winfrey on CBS, and by Larry King on CNN. Gary
Zukav appeared on *Oprah* twice. And Wayne Dyer did commentary
on MSNBC and NBC, and even had his own PBS special. All of them
gave their spiritual perspective on September 11th and introduced
their New Age/New Gospel ideas for creating peace.

As designated "spiritual experts," Williamson, Zukav, and Dyer
seemed more than eager to present their thoughts and ideas to
an American public that was searching for spiritual answers after
September 11th. Immediately challenging old mindsets, the Alliance
members were straightforward, authoritative, and even insistent
about what they said. Our world has changed, so we must change.
If we wish to "survive as a species" we need to "think differently"
about our world and about our future. We need a "new standard."
We need a "new way." We need "peace."

MARIANNE WILLIAMSON ON LARRY KING

AFTER September 11th, Marianne Williamson suddenly became one of the media "experts" being asked questions like: Why did this happen? Where was God? What can we spiritually do about it?

Larry King Live hosted Williamson on a prestigious panel of guests that included three U.S. Senators, a former Senate Majority Leader, a former Ambassador to the United Nations, and a well-known political journalist. Her inclusion on CNN's high-powered political panel was reflective of her newfound status as both spiritual and political commentator. This was emblematic of just how far she had come in the world since her first appearance on *Oprah* back in 1992.

Described by King as a "spiritual leader" and author of the book *Healing the Soul of America*, Williamson confidently told King's viewers that in regard to the events of September 11th, "Every problem comes bearing its own solution." Williamson used her prime time interview with King to introduce world peace as that solution. She explained how everyone's spirituality could be used as a "force" to help create that peace. "We have to wage peace," she emphatically stated. Speaking in generalities without actually defining her terms, Williamson made no direct mention of *A Course in Miracles*, and she made no mention of the "alternative to Armageddon" Peace Plan contained in Barbara Marx Hubbard's book, *The Revelation*. From Williamson's remarks, most viewers probably had no idea that the peace she was proposing was completely based on New Age/New Gospel principles.

Williamson's simple statement that we have to "wage peace" takes on a whole new meaning when one realizes that her ideas about peace come directly from the "Christ" of the New Age—a "Christ" who teaches that the next stage of our spiritual development is the collective realization that we are all a part of God; a "Christ" who warns that those who are unable to "move to the highest level of their nature" by acknowledging themselves as part of God will not be a part of his "peaceful" future; and a "Christ" who states that anyone opposing his peace process will be submitted to his "selection process."

Regarding September 11th, Williamson told Larry King:

> [I]t is a challenge for the human race to evolve into the next stage of our spiritual development. You know what we need to heal are the thought forms and the feelings that cause us to create war and mass destruction on this kind of a level, because ultimately if we are to survive as a species, we have to become a human race for whom the thought of war is unthinkable.
>
> We have to wage peace. . . . We need to dismantle hatred itself. And hatred is our real problem. . . . So we need to understand the spiritual malaise of hatred as much as we need to understand any of the external powers that hatred or military action we'd be involved with.
>
> . . . God would have us move to the highest level of our nature, and that means that we need to understand that our capacity to deal with the spirit—the darkness of the spirit with the light of the spirit as our greatest power.
>
> . . . We are loving each other, and in that love and that realization of our interconnectedness, we are not only finding a way to heal from the grief of what has occurred, but to endure what is occurring now and to transform what is occurring now.
>
> When the president said we have to think differently because it's a new kind of war, we have to think differently because it's a new world. We have to think differently, we have to love differently.[2]

Larry King closed the interview by telling viewers that "you always feel better" after hearing from Marianne Williamson.[3]

Marianne Williamson on Oprah

Appearing on *Oprah* soon after September 11th, Williamson emphasized her theme that "every problem comes bearing its own solution." Proposing world peace as that solution, she began introducing some of the basic concepts of her New Age/New Gospel Peace Plan, but without defining her terms. For instance, she introduced the "Atonement"—the foundational doctrine of the New Age Peace Plan—by simply stating that as individuals and as a nation we need to "atone." When Oprah asked what she meant by "atone," Williamson said that it meant that we should ask God not just to bless America but also to bless the world—asking God to heal us and to let us know what we needed to know.

Williamson's streamlined answer did not alert listeners to the New Age meaning of the "Atonement" contained in any of the 248 references in *A Course in Miracles.*[4] These references make it clear that "atoning" means seeing yourself and others as a part of God. When you "atone" you see everyone and everything as God. For instance, on page 98 of the *Course Text*, it says:

> The full awareness of the Atonement, then, is the recognition that *the separation never occurred.*

Perhaps more significantly, in terms of Williamson's discussion of peace, the New Age/New Gospel/New Spirituality teaches that peace can *only* come through the "Atonement" (at-one-ment). This is described on page 175 of the *Course Text*:

> Yet you cannot abide in peace unless you accept the Atonement, because the Atonement *is* the way to peace.

After introducing this idea of "atoning," Williamson described how she and others are gathering together in small "cell" groups ("cells of peace") to pray for world peace. Williamson explained that as people join their hearts together through meditation and prayer, they begin to create a loving "energy field" that counters the hate and negativity being generated by the world. She explained that as the number of people consciously gathering together to create peace increases, so the strength of the "forcefield" will proportionately increase. She said that prayer becomes a "conduit for miracles" as the "forcefield" grows in strength, and as the love generated from it is "harnessed" and purposefully directed for the "good" of the world.

The New Age atonement (at-one-ment) process stands in stark opposition to Jesus' atonement described in the Bible. Jesus died on the cross for all mankind. He died for us so that we might be reconciled to God (Romans 5:8–12; 2 Corinthians 5:21). (See "The Meaning of Atonement in the Bible" at the end of this chapter.)

Regarding September 11th and the need for peace and atonement, Williamson told Oprah that:

> [E]very problem comes bearing its own solution. . . . I think this tragedy has taken us to a ground of being that is like a precious vial of spiritual medicine.[5]

> So I think now we shouldn't underestimate how much good can come from just talking among ourselves, and atoning. You know, a nation atones, and I think. . . people around the world can feel us.

> . . . I've been very involved with people sitting in small groups praying, meditating and speaking from our hearts about what really matters. You know, the terrorists have cells. We hear about the terrorist cells. Well, we need cells of peace. It's not enough to just defend ourselves against violence. The greatest antidote to violence is that we proactively create fields of non-violence, fields of peace.[6]

> [W]e have a power in us more powerful than the power of bullets. The power of love can be harnessed. . . . [H]arnessing our love that it might become a social force for good. . . . Prayer is a conduit of miracles.

> . . . But love dismantles hatred, so we need [to] take our love seriously now.[7]

During the interview Williamson informed viewers that she was part of an international prayer vigil that prayed daily. She gave the time of the vigil for viewers interested in joining her peace effort. She stated that when you are involved in the prayer vigil "you feel the power." Most viewers, of course, had no idea that the "oneness" (at-one-ment) being generated from such synchronized activity provides the literal foundation for the New Age/New Gospel Peace Plan. "Christ," for example, had specifically warned Barbara Marx Hubbard that all humanity "must be consciously linked in a common thought pattern for an instant in time to AVOID ARMAGEDDON."[8]

Using a metaphor to further introduce the concept of "oneness," Williamson described how small groups of individuals around the world, consciously joined together in thought and prayer, are like the links of a chain. She gave as an example the account of the thousand or so people who miraculously escaped the World Trade Center by forming a "human chain." She suggested that we should all be like the links of that chain and that we should hold on to one another emotionally and spiritually.

Using another metaphor, Williamson further developed the New Age/New Gospel concept of "oneness." She described our country as "a fabric" and the people of our country as "the weave" of that fabric. She stated that we must be a "tight weave." She said we have become "a loose weave" and that a loose weave lets "darkness" in. She suggested that our country can become a "tight weave" as "cells of peace" build "deep community" by collectively praying, meditating, and "envisioning" a more peaceful world. She said that "fear is merely the absence of love." And that through prayer, meditation, and sharing in small groups, people find that fear is lessened.

Williamson closed her remarks on *Oprah* by stressing that "our way hasn't worked" and suggested to viewers that "there might be another way." We need to consider "new modes and new dimensions of power" in order to achieve peace. Williamson's confident and authoritative assertions left viewers with the impression that the "God" she was praying to definitely would bring peace to the world if enough people joined together to pray and meditate for that peace:

This—this is where the rubber meets the road in faith. Do we trust that as we pour spiritual power onto this, divine love onto this and ask for a miracle, one thing that this [September 11th tragedy] shows is that our way has not worked, and miracles come when we consider the possibility there might be another way. And as we sit in silence and throw divine love on to this situation and do so in community with others, that will bring forth a power out of our hearts and our consciousness and our prayers that no worldly power can express.

It's time for us to find new modes and new dimensions of power to complement worldly modes of power. That's necessary now.[9]

People who visited The Global Renaissance Alliance Web site found an Alliance "Handbook" that described how to run successful "citizen circles" ("cells of peace"). Included in the Handbook was a guided meditation for world peace as well as suggestions on how each group could best envision and pray for world peace. The Alliance Web site also contained a recommended reading list that included Williamson's book *A Return to Love: Reflections on the Principles of A Course in Miracles*, Neale Donald Walsch's *Conversations with God* books, and Barbara Marx Hubbard's book *The Revelation: A Message of Hope for the New Millennium*.[10]

GARY ZUKAV ON *OPRAH*

GLOBAL Renaissance Alliance member and best-selling New Age author Gary Zukav appeared on *Oprah* twice in the aftermath of September 11th. On both programs Zukav presented many of the same ideas previously communicated by Williamson. Using familiar New Age/New Gospel words and phrases, Zukav emphasized the need for oneness and "interconnectedness" while warning of the dangers of "separation" and "isolation." He stressed the world's need to move towards "love" and away from "fear." He also stated the need for "a new way" of looking at things, the need for "a new standard," and the need to change ourselves in order to change our world. Like Williamson, he did not define his terms. And like Williamson, he made no direct reference to the "Armageddon alternative" Peace Plan detailed in Hubbard's book *The Revelation*—a book that bears Zukav's personal endorsement on the first page.

Here are excerpts of Zukav's remarks on Oprah's post-September 11th program "Is War the Only Answer?":

> **WINFREY:** Gary Zukav is author of "The Seat of the Soul," one of my favorite books. And we've talked to him many times on this show. He also served in Vietnam as a Green Beret officer. Take a look at why Gary says that humanity is at a crossroads.

> **Mr. GARY ZUKAV (Author):** The most damaging choices that we can make are the choices of vengeance, the choices of hatred.

> . . . The hatred that exists in the world will not disappear tomorrow, and there is nothing that an Army or a Navy can do to eliminate it or even reduce it. But you can remove that energy from yourself, and in that process, you can make more intelligent decisions about how you and the United States can contribute more to the world. These events have shown us that we are interconnected through our pain, that we are not separate from others.

> . . . I have heard people say that our primary focus now should be to return to normal. That's not good enough. Our previous understanding of normal was filled with fear. . . . Our responsibility now is not to return to normal but to create a new standard for ourselves, for our country.[11]

In another post-September 11th appearance on an *Oprah* show titled "What Do You Really Believe?," Zukav again hit on the key concepts of "fear" and "separation":

These times, these events offer us opportunities to examine our belief systems and to experiment with them. Many people's belief system has been challenged by these violent and brutal events. This is good because these people are now looking inward to see whether that belief system served them.

. . . I know for sure that the universe is wise and compassionate. The question then becomes: How can there be such brutality and such pain and such suffering in our world if the universe is compassionate and wise? The reason is we put it there. We create it. And it is up to us to stop creating it.

Use those events of September 11th to begin your process of examining the parts of yourself that need to be changed, the parts that are judgmental, that are angry, the parts that bring violence into the world. We are looking for an enemy because we feel that an external enemy is the cause of the terrorism that we are frightened of. I know for sure that as we continue to look for the root of violence in other people that there will be more violence.

We cannot eliminate terror by eliminating a few people. No bomb, no bullet, no Navy or Air Force or Army will eradicate terror. This belief system that safety comes in isolation, in separation, has brought us to this collective experience of terror.

. . . Will you become more and more imprisoned by your fear? . . . We are at a turning point now because we can continue to live in fear or we can start to create a world without fear.

. . . Changing yourself is the only way that you will learn how to live a life that is without fear. As long as you are running from it, it controls you. Use these troubling times for your benefit. I know for sure that as your fears begin to leave you, your interest and care in others will increase and that your life will begin to fill with the meaning and purpose and joy that you were born to experience, that you were born to create.[12]

Most viewers would have no idea that Zukav's exhortation was really a direct challenge for them to change what they believed about God. In Zukav's New Age/New Gospel world of peace and oneness, each person must come to the eventual realization and understanding that they are a part of God. "Love" and "oneness," according to the New Age Gospel, mean seeing yourself and others as a part of God. "Fear" and "separation" mean not seeing yourself or others as a part of God.

Zukav claimed that a fear-based belief in "separation" was responsible for the "collective experience of terror" of September 11th. His inference is clear and completely consistent with the New Age position. "Fearful" people—those not seeing themselves or others as a part of God—create serious problems for everyone else because of their unbelief. "Fearful" people need to change the erroneous and harmful perception that they are "separate" and not a part of God.

In New Age/New Gospel/New Spirituality vernacular, changing yourself means remembering and realizing that you are a part of God. Everything that you think and do must flow from this concept that all is love and all is one and all is God. The New Age/New Gospel's Peace Plan is completely dependent on the world accepting "love" and "oneness" while letting go of all thought systems erroneously based in "fear" and "separation."

Wayne Dyer on PBS

Global Renaissance Alliance member Wayne Dyer made a post-September 11th appearance on PBS. His presentation of introductory New Age principles, including his enthusiastic endorsement of *A Course in Miracles*, served as an actual fundraiser for PBS itself. Although September 11th was not the main focus of his remarks, the tragic events were incorporated into the discussion and all of his material was directly relevant.

Spearheading the PBS affiliate's membership drive, Dyer's book, *There's A Spiritual Solution To Every Problem*, was offered to viewers as a premium for joining the station. His presentation was made in a colonial New England church in Concord, Massachusetts that Dyer said was once pastored by Ralph Waldo Emerson's grandfather and attended by Emerson himself. Framed in this historic setting reminiscent of the American Revolution and of our ancestors' fight for freedom, Dyer was cast in the role of a modern-day preacher.

Combining patriotism and spirituality in a style much like Marianne Williamson, Dyer told his huge PBS audience that man's "problems" arise from his belief that he is "separate" from the divine. Dyer reminded his audience that they are "one" with creation—that they are, in fact, "divine." He told them that their only problem is the mistaken belief that they are separate from their "Source":

> The other line that came to me in *A Course in Miracles*, when it uses the word "problem," said this: If you do have a problem, the only problem you have is your belief that you are separate from your Source.
>
> ... Remember, in the beginning God created heaven and earth and all that was created was good so that anything that isn't good has come about because of your belief in your mind that you are separate from this divinity. You are not what you have. You are not what you do. You are not what others think of you. You are the beloved. You are the divine. You are a creation that is made into perfection.
>
> ... When you move into a spiritual approach to life you begin to see yourself as connected to everyone and everything, and competition is replaced by something called cooperation.[13]

Combining the Prayer of Saint Francis of Assisi ("Lord make me an instrument of thy peace") with teachings from *A Course in Miracles* about peace, Dyer emphasized that peace comes from remembering one's connection to the divine. He told PBS viewers that the world would be a more peaceful place if everyone was living by the principles of *A Course in Miracles.*

> You know, I've been studying something for several years and the thing that I've been studying is called *A Course in Miracles*, and *A Course in Miracles* is a very interesting collection of brilliant writing that I think if the world were living by it perhaps we would have far, far, fewer of the conflicts and struggles and so on that we have amongst ourselves and amongst nations and in our families.[14]

THE SIGNIFICANCE OF THE CAMPAIGN

FOR years now, I have watched as New Age proponents like Marianne Williamson, Neale Donald Walsch, Benjamin Creme, Gary Zukav, Wayne Dyer, Barbara Marx Hubbard, and others have introduced the "Christ" of the New Age/New Gospel through their books and public appearances. But prior to September 11th, it was usually theoretical, and most of them seemed only loosely identified with one another.

After September 11th, everything moved into a much clearer prophetic perspective. It was extremely sobering to watch as these same individuals emerged on primetime television as part of a "global alliance" that was introducing their New Age/New Gospel/New Spirituality as a means of achieving world peace. Everything seemed to be coming together as the "God" and "Christ" of the New Age was starting to publicly introduce his "alternative to Armageddon" as the only way to a true and lasting peace.

Two Meanings of Fear Contrasted

The meaning of fear in the New Age/ New Gospel

But this paradigm shift will take great wisdom, great courage, and massive determination. For Fear will strike at the heart of these concepts and call them false. Fear will eat at the core of these magnificent truths and make them appear hollow. Fear will distort, disdain, destroy. And so Fear will be your greatest enemy. (Walsch's "God," CWG, Book 2, p. 242)

Joining the Atonement is the way out of fear. ("Jesus," ACIM Text, p. 81)

It is essential at the moment of infusion of empathy that you overcome all fear of separation from God. This overcoming of fear in a whole planetary experience is an irresistible force. No being can resist it. (Hubbard's "Christ," Revelation, pp. 244-245)

The second death, for you, is a purification, an erasing of the memory of fear, through the shock of a fire. (Hubbard's "Christ," Revelation, p. 267)

[Excerpted from: A Course in Miracles (Text); Conversations with God, Book 2 by N.D. Walsch; and The Revelation by B.M. Hubbard.]

The meaning of fear in the Bible

Fear of God

Praise ye the LORD. Blessed is the man that feareth the LORD, that delighteth greatly in his commandments. (Psalm 112:1)

Let us hear the conclusion of the whole matter: Fear God, and keep his commandments: for this is the whole duty of man. (Ecclesiastes 12:13)

The fear of the LORD is the beginning of knowledge: but fools despise wisdom and instruction. (Proverbs 1:7)

The LORD taketh pleasure in them that fear him, in those that hope in his mercy. (Psalm 147:11)

TWO MEANINGS OF FEAR CONTRASTED CONTINUED

He will fulfil the desire of them that fear him: he also will hear their cry, and will save them. (Psalm 145:19)

Behold, the eye of the LORD is upon them that fear him, upon them that hope in his mercy. (Psalm 33:18)

Be not wise in thine own eyes: fear the LORD, and depart from evil. (Proverbs 3:7)

By mercy and truth iniquity is purged: and by the fear of the LORD men depart from evil. (Proverbs 16:6)

Wherefore we receiving a kingdom which cannot be moved, let us have grace, whereby we may serve God acceptably with reverence and godly fear. (Hebrews 12:28)

HAVE NO FEAR OF MAN

In God I will praise his word, in God I have put my trust; I will not fear what flesh can do unto me. (Psalm 56:4)

The LORD is on my side; I will not fear: what can man do unto me? (Psalm 118:6)

The LORD is my light and my salvation; whom shall I fear? the LORD is the strength of my life; of whom shall I be afraid? When the wicked, even mine enemies and my foes, came upon me to eat up my flesh, they stumbled and fell. Though an host should encamp against me, my heart shall not fear: though war should rise against me, in this will I be confident. (Psalm 27:1-3)

TWO MEANINGS OF ATONEMENT CONTRASTED

THE MEANING OF ATONEMENT IN THE NEW AGE/NEW GOSPEL

The Atonement is the final lesson he [man] need learn, for it teaches him that, never having sinned, he has no need of salvation. ("Jesus," *ACIM Text*, p. 237)

The full awareness of the Atonement, then, is the recognition that *the separation never occurred.* ("Jesus," *ACIM Text*, p. 98)

You must realize that "atonement" is *just that*—it is "at-one-ment." It is the awareness that you and all others are One. It is the understanding that you are One with everything—including Me. ("God," FWG, p. 92)

The crucifixion did not establish the Atonement; the resurrection did. Many sincere Christians have misunderstood this. ("Jesus," *ACIM Text*, p. 36)

[Excerpted from: *A Course in Miracles (Text)* and *Friendship with God* by N.D. Walsch.]

THE MEANING OF ATONEMENT IN THE BIBLE

Whom God hath set forth to be a propitiation through faith in his blood, to declare his righteousness for the remission of sins that are past, through the forbearance of God. (Romans 3:25)

But God commendeth his love toward us, in that, while we were yet sinners, Christ died for us. Much more then, being now justified by his blood, we shall be saved from wrath through him. For if, when we were enemies, we were reconciled to God by the death of his Son, much more, being reconciled, we shall be saved by his life. And not only so, but we also joy in God through our Lord Jesus Christ, by whom we have now received the atonement. Wherefore, as by one man sin entered into the world, and death by sin; and so death passed upon all men, for that all have sinned. (Romans 5:8–12)

TWO MEANINGS OF ATONEMENT CONTRASTED CONTINUED

For he hath made him to be sin for us, who knew no sin; that we might be made the righteousness of God in him. (2 Corinthians 5:21)

And he is the propitiation for our sins: and not for ours only, but also for the sins of the whole world. (1 John 2:2)

Herein is love, not that we loved God, but that he loved us, and sent his Son to be the propitiation for our sins. (1 John 4:10)

Note: The definition of atonement in the New Age/New Gospel—"at-one-ment"—denies the atoning death of Jesus Christ on the cross of Calvary. The Bible, however, affirms the atoning death of Jesus Christ on the cross of Calvary.

CHAPTER EIGHT

THE ARMAGEDDON ALTERNATIVE

> And he shall magnify
> himself in his heart,
> and by peace shall
> destroy many.
> —Daniel 8:25

THERE are literally 999 references to "peace" in *A Course in Miracles*.[1] When I studied the *Course* it never occurred to me that there could be anything wrong with the peace the *Course* described or the means they prescribed for obtaining it. I believed that the "Jesus" of the *Course* had my best interests in mind when he taught me to see everyone and everything as "a part of God." I didn't know anything about spiritual deception. I didn't know that the Bible warned about a false "Christ" who would come with "signs and lying wonders" and false miracles— like the one in *A Course in Miracles*. But if you aren't familiar with the teachings of the Bible, you don't know these things. Almost everyone in this world wants love and peace. But what are the conditions necessary to obtain that love and peace? And what if the love and peace you seem to attain becomes something else down the line?

The "Christ" of the New Age/New Spirituality has a plan. He calls it "the alternative to Armageddon." He says that with his plan Armageddon can be avoided, promising that his "atonement plan" (at-one-ment plan) will work if everyone plays their necessary part. But it must be a unified team effort. One for all and all for one. There can be no detractors; there can be no weak links. "Love" and "peace" will prevail when "fear" and "separation" are overcome. "Overcomers," according to the New Age/New Gospel, are those who have overcome "fear" and "separation" by recognizing they are part of God and "at-one" with all creation.

The "Armageddon alternative" Peace Plan has been given by the false New Age "Christ" to his "avant-garde" channelers who are now in the process of gradually introducing this plan, with its underlying New Age principles, to an unsuspecting general public. But the "Armageddon alternative" is not referred to as such at this time. The terms and concepts are presented in a simple and pleasing vernacular—terms that, while loaded with hidden New Age meaning, remain non-threatening to the average person. The New Age/New Gospel Peace Plan is presented in simple sound bites about the virtues of "love," "peace," and "oneness," while warning about the dangers of "fear," "hate," "self-centeredness," and "separation." Because things are being kept purposefully vague, there is no open talk about the plan's "selection process." At least not yet.

FOUNDATIONAL BELIEFS OF THE NEW AGE PEACE PLAN

(1) Each person is a part of God. Each person is a cell in the one body of God that is humanity. Each person (cell) is divinely interconnected through their "God-self," "Christ-self," or "Higher self" to one another.

(2) Fear-based belief systems (like biblical "old Gospel" Christianity) deny that we are a part of God. This denial creates the illusion that humanity, the world, and God are *separate* from self. This "misperception" creates a world that is filled with self-centeredness, violence, hate, and war.

(3) Love-based belief systems (like New Age/New Gospel teachings) affirm that we *are* a part of God. This affirmation results in the new perception that humanity, the world, and God are "one" with self. This new perception creates a world that is filled with selflessness, non-violence, love, and peace.

(4) Whatever we think is what we draw to ourselves. If we believe that war is inevitable, then the power of that belief will make it so. If we believe that peace is inevitable, then the power of that belief will make it so.

(5) For the Peace Plan to work, each person must responsibly play their part in the "peace process." Those who do not responsibly play their part hinder the evolution of humanity and the attainment of peace.

How the New Age Peace Plan Will Be Enacted

(1) Each person must recognize that the world is in great peril; if something isn't done soon, humanity as a species could become extinct.

(2) Each person as a cell in the one body of humanity that is God has a responsibility to function properly within the context of the body by thinking "right" thoughts, and relating to the body in a unified, wholistic manner.

(3) Each person understands that the future of the world is up to the collective body. What they think is what they get. Thoughts of love, unity, and peace must prevail.

(4) Each person must correct any "misperception" that reinforces the idea that God, self, humanity, and the world are separate from one another. All fear-based notions of *separateness* must be eliminated from their thoughts and actions. No more separatist thoughts about sin, Satan, or Armageddon being real. Only thoughts of God, love, and peace.

(5) Through prayer and meditation each person begins to envision and create the peaceful world they would like to see. They affirm and hold that vision of peace in their daily thoughts.

(6) People gather together in small groups to increase the power of their individual envisioning. They join together as an expression of their oneness to collectively pray and meditate and hold the vision of a peaceful world.

(7) People meditate, pray, and hold the vision of peace at the same time around the world to increase the power of their effort.

(8) Special events are arranged where people around the world can link more openly with one another (like the 1987 Harmonic Convergence) to increase the power of their collective vision. People begin to see and experience the power that comes from joining together in expressions of "oneness." (Barbara Marx Hubbard was in Boulder, Colorado with the originator of the Harmonic Convergence, Jose Arguelles during the 1987 event.[2])

9) As humanity becomes more aligned within its one body and unified in its expressed desire for peace, the power of God is more flowing and present, and there is an increase in miracles and healings.

10) As everyone links through their "God-self," "Christ-self," or "Higher self," the power of God (i.e., the "Force") begins to manifest its presence.

(11) Only fear, with its illusion of *separateness*, can threaten the flow of the "Force" within the one body and keep the body from experiencing feelings of peace and oneness. These thoughts of *separation* are like cancer cells in the body and must be completely healed or "removed" from the body.

(12) Because thoughts of *separation* threaten the health and the peace of the body, a system is devised to visibly mark those who recognize their oneness with God. Those who do not submit to the process ultimately reveal themselves as separatists.

(13) An appointed day arrives when all of those who want the God and Christ potentials within them to be fully activated align themselves in a designated moment in time with all humanity.

(14) With the "Force" of God fully manifesting in one moment through all mankind, humanity experiences itself as the "one body" of God.

(15) This universal link-up with the "Force" results in all humanity being resurrected—lifted up and born again into a whole new way of being. In the twinkling of an eye, they are taken to a new spiritual level as they now actually experience themselves as a part of God.

(16) Once humanity has been linked as "one" and corporately transformed, Christ, and ultimately God, will be enabled to "return" to earth. Peace will reign in the "New Heaven," on the "New Earth," and in the "New Jerusalem." Projects of goodwill shall prevail. *Sharing* will be the key word.

(17) Self-centered and separatist members of the "one body" who choose not to participate in this transformational Peace Plan will be judged and removed from the corporate body by the "selection process." Separatists are not allowed to hinder the spiritual development of the rest of the "one body." They will not be allowed to keep peace from happening. They are removed for the good of all.

Just as Global Renaissance Alliance members appeared on primetime television after September 11th, it is expected that they will become even more of a presence during any future crises. Convinced that their "Christ" has a way to save the world from disaster, they will continue to introduce his New Age/New Gospel Peace Plan to a world that is desperate for peace—a Peace Plan that their "Christ" has described in detail as the "alternative to Armageddon."

THE ARMAGEDDON ALTERNATIVE: THE PLANETARY PENTECOST

DIRECT QUOTES FROM HUBBARD'S "CHRIST" IN *THE REVELATION*

The alternative to Armageddon is the Planetary Pentecost. When a critical mass is in the upper room of consciousness on a planetary scale, each will hear from within, in their own language, the mighty words of God. All who are attuned will be radically empowered to be and do as Jesus did. (p. 157)

Here we are, now poised either on the brink of destruction greater than the world has ever seen—a destruction which will cripple planet Earth forever and release only the few to go on—or on the threshold of global co-creation wherein each person on Earth will be attracted to participate in his or her own evolution to godliness. (p. 174)

It [Armageddon] will be a self-fulfilling prophecy if we force ourselves to continue contemplating this disastrous set of events. (p. 204)

Armageddon is, dearly beloved, the dreadful script which you and I rewrite now. (p. 204)

This text was written not to add or subtract from the divine book of Revelation. It was written to inform you of the alternative to Armageddon. (p. 305)

The Book of Revelation is a description of one path to the New Jerusalem, but this scenario is not inevitable. (p. 158)

The Book of Revelation [in the Bible] describes the violent path to the New Jerusalem. This *Revelation* [Hubbard's book] describes the loving path to the same condition. (p. 265)

You are to prepare the way for the alternative to Armageddon, which is the Planetary Pentecost, the great Instant of Co-operation which can transform enough, en masse, to avoid the necessity of the seventh seal being broken. (pp. 172–173)

Tell them to recognize the God within themselves, and to follow that light through the darkness of the tribulations to the dawn of the Universal Age, when only the God-conscious continue to exist, and everyone is like Christ. (p. 102)

You are to provide the opportunity for a planetary signal wherein each person who chooses life over death can register that decision visibly—a coming to witness before the world. (p. 302)

Each shall be "sealed" with the seal of the living God. This means that they shall be marked, visibly identified, first to themselves, then to others. (p. 149)

All those sealed with the seal of the living God must be consciously linked in a common thought pattern for an instant in time to AVOID ARMAGEDDON. The bell will never toll, if you can link before the end must come. (p. 241)

Those with the seal of the living God on their foreheads will be with Christ at the time of the Transformation. (p. 190)

I cannot "return" until enough of you are attracted and linked. (p. 66)

There will be practices for this coming event. (p. 242)

Either the good will prevail, connect, link, and magnetize the majority of humanity to act with love for life everlasting, or the violent selection of the self-centered will begin. (p. 303)

The decisive moment of selection has almost come. The judgment of the quick and the dead is about to be made. The end of this phase of evolution is nearly complete. (p. 189)

All who choose life everlasting have judged themselves worthy to be me. (p. 304)

If those people who are not self-centered align their thoughts in perfect faith, that they are whole, created in the image of God, the world can be saved. (p. 157)

As the Planetary Smile ripples through the nervous systems of earth and the Instant of Co-operation begins, empathy floods the feelings of the whole body of Earth, separateness is overcome, and I appear to all of you at once. (p. 245)

ARMAGEDDON ALTERNATIVE CONTINUED

At the moment of cosmic contact, I will appear to you both through inner experience and through external communication in your mass media—the nervous system of the world. You will all feel, hear, and see my presence at one instant in time, each in your own way. (p. 245)

An uncontrollable joy will ripple through the thinking layer of Earth. The co-creative systems, which are lying psychologically dormant in humanity will be activated. From within, all sensitive persons will feel the joy of the force, flooding their systems with love and attraction. It will be as irresistible as sex. (p. 243)

As this joy flashes through the nervous systems of the most sensitive peoples on Earth, it will create a psycho-magnetic field of empathy, which will align the next wave of people in synchrony, everywhere on Earth. This massive, sudden empathic alignment will cause a shift in the consciousness of Earth. (p. 243)

It is essential at the moment of infusion of empathy that you overcome all fear of separation from God. This overcoming of fear in a whole planetary experience is an irresistible force. No being can resist it. (pp. 244-245)

The cancer of self-centeredness will be consumed by the experience of wholeness. (p. 245)

At the time of the Quantum Instant there will be a judgment of the quick and the dead. That is, there will be an evolutionary selection process based on your qualifications for co-creative power. (p. 111)

The species known as self-centered humanity will become extinct. The species known as whole-centered humanity will evolve. (p. 111)

After the selection process, you will be born to the next stage of evolution. There will be a New Heaven, a New Earth, a new body and a new consciousness for all who survive. (p. 261)

The New Jerusalem is the new city which emerges naturally from a New Heaven and a New Earth. It is the human community as a collectivity of natural Christs. (p. 258)

ARMAGEDDON ALTERNATIVE CONTINUED

I will write upon you my new name, which is not the Master Jesus who went to the cross but the risen Christ who arose from the dead. (p. 115)

Those who choose this version of the future will be there. Those who do not choose it will not be there. Choose well, dearly beloved, choose well. (p. 288)

THE MARK

THE MARK OF THE BEAST
And he causeth all, both small and great, rich and poor, free and bond, to receive a mark in their right hand, or in their foreheads: And that no man might buy or sell, save he that had the mark, or the name of the beast, or the number of his name. (Revelation 13:16–17)

DIRECT QUOTES FROM HUBBARD'S "CHRIST" IN *THE REVELATION*

You are to provide the opportunity for a planetary signal wherein each person who chooses life over death can register that decision visibly—a coming to witness before the world. (p. 302)

Each shall be "sealed" with the seal of the living God. This means that they shall be marked, visibly identified, first to themselves, then to others. This

means that their inner eye in the forehead will be fully opened by this touch, henceforth awakening them from the womb of self-centeredness. (p. 149)

I will write upon you my new name, which is not the Master Jesus who went to the cross but the risen Christ who arose from the dead, ascended into heaven, and sits at the right hand of God. (p. 115)

Those who have the seal of the living God will be able to take the next step of evolution. (p. 150)

Those with the seal of the living God on their foreheads will be with Christ at the time of the Transformation. (p. 190)

This critical mass represents those marked with the seal of the living God on their foreheads. (p. 198)

FURTHER PROPHETIC SIGNS

THE BIBLE'S PROPHETIC WARNING

Now the Spirit speaketh expressly, that in the latter times some shall depart from the faith, giving heed to seducing spirits, and doctrines of devils; Speaking lies in hypocrisy; having their conscience seared with a hot iron; Forbidding to marry, and commanding to abstain from meats, which God hath created to be received with thanksgiving of them which believe and know the truth. (1 Timothy 4:1-3)

NEW AGE/NEW GOSPEL QUOTES UNDERMINING MARRIAGE

In the future our partners will be chosen in a much more scientific way, according to Ray quality, karmic relationship, and point in evolution. (Creme, *Reappearance*, p. 185)

Fidelity of the partners is to each other for the sake of their chosen act, whether it be a godly child or godly work in the universe.

When the act is completed, the partnership is renewed if there is more to be done. It is lovingly ended if there is nothing more to be created by that particular couple. Each discovers the next partner, or partners, with no hint of sorrow, for nothing is separated among those totally connected with God. (Hubbard's "Christ," *Revelation*, p. 166)

No sexual reproduction, only conscious conceptions. . . . (Hubbard's "Christ,"*Revelation*, p. 283)

You will choose to create another being only on very special occasions when the whole community of natural Christs sees the requirement. The selection of the individual to be embodied is done by conscious selection. (Hubbard's "Christ," *Revelation*, p. 165)

Walsch: So are You saying that marriage should go?
"God": I have no preference in the matter. (*CWG Book 3*, p. 219)

FURTHER PROPHETIC SIGNS CONTINUED

ABSTAINING FROM MEATS

The defect of carnivorous behavior will gradually be overcome. Eating meat will cease. (Hubbard's "Christ," *Revelation*, p. 263)

There are two defects from which you suffer, carnivorous behavior and the illusion of separation from God. (Hubbard's "Christ,"*Revelation*, p. 187)

But in the New Age vegetarianism will become the norm. (Creme, *Reappearance*, p. 194)

[Excerpted from: *Conversations with God: Book 3*, N.D. Walsch; *The Reappearance of the Christ and the Masters of Wisdom*, B. Creme; and *The Revelation*, B.M. Hubbard.]

Yea, and all that will live godly in Christ Jesus shall suffer persecution.

—2 Timothy 3:12

CHAPTER NINE

THE NEW AGE DOCTRINE OF SEPARATION

Blessed are ye, when men shall hate you, and when they shall separate you from their company, and shall reproach you, and cast out your name as evil, for the Son of man's sake. — Luke 6:22

IN the New Age scheme of things "love" means seeing yourself and your fellow man as a part of God and "one" with God. "Love" and "oneness" are equated with all of those who confess themselves to be a part of God. "Love" and "oneness" are said to be true perceptions based on right thinking. "Love" and "oneness" produce peace, health, and spiritual growth in the "one body" of mankind. They are the ticket to the next spiritual level. "Love" and "oneness" people are those who follow New Age/New Gospel teachings and the New Age God and Christ.

In the New Age Gospel scheme of things, "fear" means seeing yourself and your fellow man as "separate" and not as a part of God. "Fear" and "separation" are equated with all of those who refuse to see themselves as being a part of God. "Fear" and "separation" are said to be erroneous perceptions based on wrong thinking. "Fear" and "separation" prevent the attainment of peace, produce illness in the body of mankind, and prevent spiritual growth. They are the ticket to the "selection process" because they prevent the "one body" of humanity from advancing to the next spiritual level. "Fear" and "separation" people are those who oppose New Age/New Gospel teachings and the New Age God and Christ. Traditional Christian believers, by New Age definition, are "fear" and "separation" people.

The "God" and "Christ" of the New Age Spirituality use these cleverly contrived words and concepts to divide the world into two camps: those who follow them and those who oppose them. Through the ingenious use of language they make their case and push their position. Always taking the high road of "love" and "oneness" they isolate those who oppose them by branding them as "fearful" and "separate."

The "God" and "Christ" of the New Age/New Gospel are very adept at never saying "traditional Christian believers," but instead say "those who are under the illusion of separation." They do not say "traditional Christianity is evil" or "traditional Christianity is of the devil." They say "separation is evil" and "separation is of the devil." Instead of saying, "traditional Christianity is a crime that must be driven from this world," they state: "The crime of separation must be driven from this world."[1] Instead of saying, "traditional Christian believers will one day be submitted to the selection process," they state: "All that hinders the manifestation of man's divinity must be driven from our planet."[2]

How do the New Age "God" and "Christ" suggest that Christians, and others under "the illusion of separation," rid themselves of the "fear" that is causing them to feel separate from God? By "atoning" through the "at-one-ment" process. That is, by affirming that "all is love" and "all is God" and never forgetting that they are a part of God. By their definition, the only way you can be "loving" and "at-one" with your fellow man is by ultimately pledging allegiance to the doctrine of "oneness." From this perspective you are either a "love" and "oneness" person or you are a "fear" and "separation" person. Your "love" of God is expressed by seeing yourself and others as a part of God, as "one" with God. Your "fear" of God is expressed by seeing yourself and others as not being a part of God, as "separate" from God. In their New Age future, you will live or die based on whether or not you see yourself as a part of God. It is the doctrine of "oneness" versus the doctrine of "separation." It is as simple and straightforward and brutal as that.

If it all sounds kind of backward, that is because it is. It is the language and methodology of the "God" and "Christ" of the New Age/New Gospel. And it is the same terminology and methodology being used by their New Age followers. "Oneness" is presented as the inevitable by-product of "love" and as such is like "mom and apple pie." Who could possibly be against "mom and apple pie"? "Separateness" is regarded as the inevitable by-product of "fear" and as such is like "the Grinch who stole Christmas." Who in their right mind supports "the Grinch who stole Christmas"? The upshot of this clever conditioning process is to impress people everywhere with the seemingly indisputable contention that if you are against "oneness" you are also against God, Christ, and your fellow man.

> In their New Age future, you will live or die based on whether or not you see yourself as a part of God.

Only an ingenious and creatively deceptive spirit world could have thought up such a diabolical way of separating and disparaging Christian believers and others who do not believe they are a part of God. Who could possibly be against "oneness"? And the answer is, of course, only those who have been "deceived" into believing in "the crime of separation." Only those who are under the "self-centered" illusion that they are "separate" and not a part of God. Only those who have been "deluded" into believing that the "sin of separation" is real.

THE HOSTILE NEW GOSPEL

IT is ironic that New Age/New Gospel advocates present themselves as being so loving, tolerant, and accepting of all major religions. "God" told Neale Donald Walsch, "There are a thousand paths to God, and every one gets you there."[3] But "God" conveniently overlooks telling Walsch's readers about a detour called the "selection process" for those who insist on being "separate" and "self-centered"—the "shock of a fire" and "a second death" for those who refuse to bow down to the doctrine of "oneness" and the "God" and "Christ" of the New Age/New Gospel.

New Age matriarch Alice Bailey was told by her spirit guide over fifty years ago that the "Forces of Darkness" would oppose the New Age. These "Forces" are described as being spiritually blind and characterized by "separateness" and "hate."

> The Forces of Darkness are powerful energies. . . . They consequently block deliberately the inflow of that which is new and life-giving; they work to prevent the understanding of that which is of the New Age; they endeavor to preserve that which is familiar and old, to counteract the effects of the oncoming culture and civilization, to bring blindness to the peoples and to feed steadily the existing fires of hate, of separateness, of criticism and of cruelty.[4]

"God" warns Walsch about the fearful people who will try to undermine his "magnificent truths" by calling them false, saying they will be "your greatest enemy."

> But this paradigm shift will take great wisdom, great courage, and massive determination. For Fear will strike at the heart of these concepts and call them false. Fear will eat at the core of these magnificent truths and make them appear hollow. Fear will distort, disdain, destroy. And so Fear will be your greatest enemy.[5]

The New Age/New Gospel/New Spirituality is anything but loving, tolerant, and accepting towards those who oppose it. The "Christ" of the New Age Gospel warns that those who are "fearful" are "separate" and "self-centered." He declares that "separate" and "self-centered" people must ultimately be handed over to the "selection process." He declares that "separate" and "self-centered" people must ultimately be removed from the planet.

> The recognition of God is the recognition of yourself. There is no separation of God and His creation.[6]

> . . . [T]he fundamental regression is self-centeredness, or the illusion that you are separate from God. I "make war" on self-centeredness.[7]

> At the co-creative stage of evolution, one self-centered soul is like a lethal cancer cell in a body: deadly to itself and to the whole.[8]

> The surgeon dare leave no cancer in the body when he closes up the wound after a delicate operation. We dare leave no self-centeredness on Earth after the selection process.[9]

> The species known as self-centered humanity will become extinct. The species known as whole-centered humanity will evolve.[10]

The section on the next page reveals just how intolerant and unloving the "God" and "Christ" of the New Age are toward traditional Christian believers and all others who refuse to see themselves as a part of God.

THE MEANING OF "SEPARATION" IN THE NEW AGE GOSPEL

DIRECT QUOTES FROM "GOD" OR "CHRIST"

SEPARATION IS AN ILLUSION

This is your assignment. This is your work. You are to destroy the illusion of separation. (Walsch's "God," *FWG*, p. 21)

SEPARATION IS NOT BELIEVING YOU ARE A PART OF GOD

The recognition of God is the recognition of yourself. There is no separation of God and His creation. ("Jesus," *ACIM Text*, p. 147)

Nothing separates you from Me, and soon many will realise this. I am with you and in you. I seek to express That which I am through you; for this I come. (Maitreya, *Messages*, p. 22)

SEPARATION IS SELF-CENTEREDNESS

[T]he fundamental regression is self-centeredness, or the illusion that you are separate from God. I "make war" on self-centeredness. It shall surely be overcome. The child must become the adult. Human must become Divine. That is the law. (Hubbard's "Christ," *Revelation*, p. 233)

SEPARATION IS NOT LOVE

Love is the only way. You cannot gain the next stage of evolution in a self-centered state. (Hubbard's "Christ," *Revelation*, p. 236)

SEPARATION IS FEAR

It is essential at the moment of infusion of empathy that you overcome all fear of separation from God. This overcoming of fear in a whole planetary experience is an irresistible force. No being can resist it. (Hubbard's "Christ," *Revelation*, pp. 244–245)

SEPARATION IS HATRED

Let us together show the world: that the need for war is past; that the instinct of man is to live and to love; that hatred is begotten of separation. . . . (Maitreya, *Messages*, p. 108)

SEPARATION IS EVIL

Just before the final wave of tribulations—the seven last plagues—those who resist evil, those who are victorious in their struggle against the temptation of separation, stand upon a burning sea of glass. (Hubbard's "Christ," *Revelation*, p. 201)

MEANING OF "SEPARATION" CONTINUED

SEPARATION IS SATAN

When at last you see that there is no separation in God's World—that is, nothing which is not God—then, at last, will you let go of this invention of man which you have called Satan. (Walsch's "God," *CWG Book 3*, p. 56)

The mind can make the belief in separation very real and very fearful, and this belief *is* the "devil." ("Jesus," *ACIM Text*, p. 50)

Your triumph over Satan, that is, over the illusion of separation, will be a victory for the universal community. (Hubbard's "Christ," *Revelation*, p. 193)

SEPARATION IS SIN

I shall drive from this Earth forever the curse of hatred, the sin of separation. (Maitreya, *Messages*, p. 104)

SEPARATION IS SICKNESS

A sick person perceives himself as separate from God. Would you see him as separate from you? It is your task to heal the sense of separation that has made him sick. ("Jesus," *ACIM Manual*, p. 56)

SEPARATION IS LAWLESSNESS

The crime of separation, of division, of lawlessness must go from the world. All that hinders the manifestation of man's divinity must be driven from our planet. My Law will take the place of separation. (Maitreya, *Messages*, p. 248)

SEPARATION IS CRIME

The crime of separation must be driven from this world. I affirm that as My Purpose. (Maitreya, *Messages*, p. 189)

SEPARATION IS A "LACK" THAT MUST BE CORRECTED

A sense of separation from God is the only lack you really need correct. ("Jesus," *ACIM Text*, p. 14)

[Excerpted from: *A Course in Miracles*; *Conversations with God, Book 3* and *Friendship with God*, N.D. Walsch; *Messages from Maitreya the Christ*; and *The Revelation*, B.M. Hubbard.]

THE BIBLE'S MEANING OF SEPARATION FROM GOD

Note: Man, by his selfish choice to disobey God in the Garden of Eden, willingly chose the path that would separate him from fellowship with God. At that moment sin, death, shame, fear, guilt—all the things that plague the human race—were introduced to the human soul that had, to that point known Divine fellowship and love. The response of the Lord was to seek the lost. Then, as now, God is at work, redeeming our separation by atoning sacrifice, which is a gift of His love to His creation. Jesus Christ came to seek and redeem the lost (the separated). Those who acknowledge their need are brought back into fellowship with God through Jesus' atonement. At Christ's death, the veil of "separation" in the temple was torn in two (Matthew 27:50-51), ending sin's separating curse once and for all. The root of the sin that separates man and God has always been born first in the concept "I will" (self). The mistake of deifying the creature/creation as opposed to worshipping the Creator has always provoked judgment/separation from God.[11]

SEPARATION IS A RESULT OF WORSHIPPING CREATION

Because that, when they knew God, they glorified him not as God, neither were thankful; but became vain in their imaginations, and their foolish heart was darkened. Professing themselves to be wise, they became fools, And changed the glory of the uncorruptible God into an image made like to corruptible man, and to birds, and fourfooted beasts, and creeping things. Wherefore God also gave them up to uncleanness through the lusts of their own hearts, to dishonour their own bodies between themselves: Who changed the truth of God into a lie, and worshipped and served the creature more than the Creator, who is blessed for ever. Amen. (Romans 1:21-25)

SEPARATION IS ENDED BY ATONEMENT OF JESUS CHRIST

For if, when we were enemies, we were reconciled to God by the death of his Son, much more, being reconciled, we shall be saved by his life. And not only so, but we also joy in God through our Lord Jesus Christ, by whom we have now received the atonement. (Romans 5:10-11)

That at that time ye were without Christ, being aliens from the commonwealth of Israel, and strangers from the covenants of

THE BIBLE'S MEANING CONTINUED

promise, having no hope, and without God in the world: But now in Christ Jesus ye who sometimes were far off are made nigh by the blood of Christ. For he is our peace, who hath made both one, and hath broken down the middle wall of partition between us ... For through him we both have access by one Spirit unto the Father. Now therefore ye are no more strangers and foreigners, but fellow citizens with the saints, and of the household of God. (Ephesians 2:12-14, 18-19)

BELIEVERS CANNOT BE SEPARATED FROM JESUS CHRIST

For I am persuaded, that neither death, nor life, nor angels, nor principalities, nor powers, nor things present, nor things to come, nor height, nor depth, nor any other creature, shall be able to separate us from the love of God, which is in Christ Jesus our Lord. (Romans 8:38-39)

BELIEVERS ARE HATED AND SEPARATED BY THE WORLD

Blessed are ye, when men shall hate you, and when they shall separate you from their company, and shall reproach you, and cast out your name as evil, for the Son of man's sake. (Luke 6:22)

If ye were of the world, the world would love his own: but because ye are not of the world, but I have chosen you out of the world, therefore the world hateth you. (John 15:19)

I have given them thy word; and the world hath hated them, because they are not of the world, even as I am not of the world. I pray not that thou shouldest take them out of the world, but that thou shouldest keep them from the evil. (John 17:14-15)

BELIEVERS SEPARATE THEM-SELVES FROM THE WORLD

Enter ye in at the strait gate: for wide is the gate, and broad is the way, that leadeth to destruction, and many there be which go in thereat: Because strait is the gate, and narrow is the way, which leadeth unto life, and few there be that find it. (Matthew 7:13-14)

Wherefore come out from among them, and be ye separate, saith the Lord, and touch not the unclean thing; and I will receive you. (2 Corinthians 6:17)

CHAPTER TEN

THE SILENT CHURCH

> But while men slept, his enemy came
> and sowed tares among the wheat, and
> went his way. — Matthew 13:25

MANY Christian believers smirked when Shirley MacLaine stood on the beach in her made-for-TV movie, *Out on a Limb*, exclaiming, "I am God!" Yet Marianne Williamson exclaimed that we are all "God" and was introduced by Tom Brokaw on a primetime NBC special report about September 11th as one of our "religious leaders."[1] Gary Zukav, a man who personally endorsed the Barbara Marx Hubbard book, *The Revelation*, that describes the "selection process," told us in his post-September 11th television appearances how we can all spiritually grow and bring peace to the world. And Wayne Dyer, in a post-September 11th PBS fundraising event, stood in a historic New England church and told his national audience that the world would be a much more peaceful place if everyone adopted the "brilliant" teachings of *A Course in Miracles*.

Traditional Christian believers frequently mention the analogy of the frog that is so slowly and gradually boiled in a kettle of water that it dies before ever realizing what is going on. Yet many believers fail to realize that the very same thing is happening to them as they tell that story. How else do you explain the rapid rise of the New Age/New Gospel/ New Spirituality movement with hardly a word of concern within the

Church about what's been happening? As New Age advocates continue to publish best-selling books and flock to the airwaves in ever-increasing numbers to advance their cause, there is a strange silence in Christendom. Does the Church have any idea what is going on?

So often we have heard the impassioned refrain, "We can never let what happened in Germany ever happen again." And with all of the Holocaust memorials, survivor testimonies, and multitudinous books on the subject, we have done a pretty good job of convincing ourselves that we will never make the same mistakes the German people did in allowing someone like Hitler to rise in their midst. We think that Americans would never stand by and allow something like that to happen here in our country. Our democratic processes and old-fashioned common sense would never allow it.

> Christians don't seem to grasp Jesus' warnings about the tremendous deception that characterizes the time of the end.

In the introduction to a 1999 publication (Sixth Pressing) of Hitler's *Mein Kampf*, Konrad Heiden describes how everything that Hitler was about to do was telegraphed in his early writings:

> For years *Mein Kampf* stood as proof of the blindness and complacency of the world. For in its pages Hitler announced—long before he came to power—a program of blood and terror in a self-revelation of such overwhelming frankness that few among its readers had the courage to believe it. Once again it was demonstrated that there was no more effective method of concealment than the broadest publicity.[2]

Somehow, Christians don't seem to grasp Jesus' warnings about the tremendous deception that characterizes the time of the end. Perhaps deceived into thinking that we can't be deceived, we don't take seriously enough His warnings that a Hitler-like Antichrist figure will one day rise to rule the world—and that many people calling themselves "Christians" will support this spiritual counterfeit who will actually come in the name of Christ. Our adversary wants us to believe that these warnings are for another people at another time. Yet through Scripture, and in our heart of hearts, the Spirit of God tells us that they are not. As we study the Bible, and as we watch and pray and observe the events all around us, we come to understand that these future times described by Jesus are now suddenly and undeniably upon us.

GRIEVOUS WOLVES

IN his second letter to the Corinthians, Paul warns of their vulnerability and susceptibility to false teaching in the name of Jesus. He suggests that if someone approached them with "another gospel," "another Jesus," and "another spirit" they might very well go along with it (2 Corinthians 11:3-4). Earlier in that same letter Paul had indirectly encouraged the Corinthians not to be ignorant of their adversary's schemes and devices, lest they be taken advantage of (2 Corinthians 2:11). Paul told the Ephesians that "it is a shame" that we even have to talk about the things of darkness, but when we expose them they are brought into the light (Ephesians 5:12-13). He also told them that he had not ceased to warn them night and day for three years that men who were "grievous wolves" would "arise" in the Church "speaking perverse things" as they attempted to lead men away from their faith and into the enemy's camp (Acts 20:29-31). Let us beware of these same warnings today.

It is extremely disturbing to see the Web site of a Colorado-based Christian leader listed as a recommended resource in the back of a 1998 Barbara Marx Hubbard book titled *Conscious Evolution*.[3] It is equally alarming to find out that this individual was also a member of the same World Future Society that lists Barbara Marx Hubbard as one of its co-founding and current board members[4]—and that this respected Christian leader served as the secretary of a World Future Society subcommittee that once gave Hubbard a special award for her outstanding contributions to the field of religion.[5] But perhaps what is most unbelievable is that Christian leadership let him get away with it. Apparently, being "yoked" with a woman who (at the direction of her "Christ") has re-written the Book of Revelation and authored the "selection process" is not a major concern for church leaders—leaders who are actually starting to sound a lot like Hubbard themselves.

And it is, indeed, very disturbing to see many Christian leaders today using many of the same words and expressions commonly used by their New Age/New Gospel counterparts. "New revelation" describing how a great "move of God" is going to take believers "pregnant with destiny" to "a new spiritual level" and into a "new dimension" sounds a lot more like the New Age than the traditional Gospel of Jesus Christ.

WHERE IS THE CHURCH HEADING?

ARE Christian leaders leading the church ever closer to the cross, or ever closer to the "Planetary Pentecost"? Why is there almost no call for spiritual discernment within the Church (except to warn believers not to be deceived into doubting their appointed Christian leaders)? Why is spiritual experience taking precedence over spiritual discernment? Why are there so few warnings about a counterfeit New Age/New Spirituality movement that maligns the person of Jesus Christ and threatens the lives of His followers? Why is "new revelation" in many ministries starting to supersede God's written Word? Why are Christians only being prepared for blessings and not for persecution? What in the world is going on?

Expecting only revival and the return of the true Christ, will people calling themselves Christians be deceived by the one who will come in the name of Christ and pretend to be Him? Caught unawares, will they mistake the counterfeit Christ's "Planetary Pentecost" for the great

> Why is there almost no call for spiritual discernment within the Church (except to warn believers not to be deceived into doubting their appointed Christian leaders)?

"move of God" they had been told to expect? Is this all a set up for the great delusion described in the Bible? Is there any good reason to not at least consider this possibility?

The prophet Daniel makes mention of the God of "forces" in conjunction with Antichrist (Daniel 11:38). The "God" of the New Age/New Gospel asks Neale Donald Walsch, "What if I am not a 'man' at all, but rather, a Force?"[6] The "Christ" of *A Course in Miracles* states that there is an "irresistible Force" within each person.[7] Marianne Williamson explains that this "universal force" can be "activated" within each person and has "the power to make all things right."[8] The New Age "Christ" tells Barbara Marx Hubbard that on the day of "Planetary Pentecost" a "Planetary Smile" will flash across the face of all mankind; that an "uncontrollable joy" that he describes as the "joy of the force" will "ripple" through the one body of humanity.[9] Benjamin Creme describes the event as "a Pentecostal experience for all."[10] The "Christ" of *A Course in Miracles* tells how the world ends in "peace" and "laughter."[11]

Has anyone wondered whether this same "Force" may be counterfeiting the Holy Spirit in churches and may be producing revivals and moves of God that are not really revivals or moves of God at all? Is the "God of forces" in the process of preparing a deceived Church for the "Planetary Pentecost"? Should we not be doing a more thorough job of testing the spirits (1 John 4:1-3)? Have we put our faith and trust in Christian "leaders" rather than in God? Have we all talked ourselves out of the end times? Have we all agreed that persecution is not something we need to be concerned about? Have we prayed to God that we would not be deluded or deceived?

In my book, *The Light That Was Dark*, I wrote the following:

> Clearly, many who said they were of "the faith" would soon become a part of the deception too, if they weren't already.

> Were we witnessing the great "falling away" predicted in the Bible (2 Thessalonians 2:3)? Was the "mystery of iniquity" talked about in the Scriptures already doing its deceptive work with "all power and signs and lying

wonders" and "all deceivableness of unrighteousness" (2 Thessalonians 2:7-10)? Would people calling themselves Christians abandon their faith in the Bible and the Bible's Christ (1 Timothy 4:1)? Would they join an ecumenical movement that in the name of love, God, unity, and peace would sacrifice the truth of the Bible and perhaps one day merge with the New Age itself? Jesus warned that such a faith would lead not to life but to ultimate destruction:

> Enter ye in at the strait gate: for wide is the gate, and broad is the way, that leadeth to destruction, and many there be which go in thereat: Because strait is the gate, and narrow is the way, which leadeth unto life, and few there be that find it. (Matthew 7:13-14)[12]

Could it be that the reason the Church is so unaware of the New Age/New Gospel movement is because it is being led by that same spirit and heading down that same broad way? Is it happening now, right in front of our very own eyes?

"THE FORCE"

But in his estate shall he [Antichrist] honour the God of forces. Daniel 11:38

DIRECT QUOTES FROM THE NEW AGE "GOD" AND "CHRIST"

Many around Me now have recognised Me, work with Me and channel My Force. (Maitreya, *Messages*, p. 262)

You cannot do it by human will and desire alone. You are to be empowered by the force that creates the universe. ("Christ," *Revelation*, p. 94)

You are letting the force be with you! And that is good. That is very good. For as you move into the next millennium, you will plant the seeds of the greatest growth the world has ever seen. ("God," *FWG*, p. 295)

Many now are awake to these divine aspects, and call for the restructuring of your world. My Force is behind them. (Maitreya, *Messages*, p. 276)

What if I am not a "man" at all, but rather, a Force, an "Energy" in the universe, that IS the universe, and that is, in fact, All That Is. What if I am The Collective? ("God," *CWG Book 3*, p. 325)

Walsch: "May the force be with you."
"God": Precisely. Do you think George Lucas came up with that by accident? (*FWG*, p. 228)

[Instant of] Co-operation does not mean being nice to each other.... It means co-operating with God. It means co-evolving with me. It means all of you co-experiencing the same force at the same time and acting together in accord with the idea that you all have from within. ("Christ," *Revelation*, p. 244)

An uncontrollable joy will ripple through the thinking layer of Earth. The co-creative systems, which are lying psychologically dormant in humanity will be activated. From within, all sensitive persons will feel the joy of the force, flooding their systems with love and attraction. ("Christ," *Revelation*, p. 243)

"THE FORCE" CONTINUED

At the next stage of evolution, life is a constant choice. If you falter in your choice to live as a son or daughter of God, you experience disconnection from the force. At the Christ-stage of existence you cannot forget who you are—and continue to live at that stage. ("Christ," *Revelation*, p. 101)

Yet within you is a Force that no illusions can resist. ("Jesus," ACIM *Text*, p. 479)

EXPERIENCE VS. THE WORD

DIRECT QUOTES FROM NEW AGE AUTHORS

What the orthodox theologian and the narrow doctrinaire have to offer no longer satisfies the intelligent seeker or suffices to answer his questions; he is shifting his allegiances into wider and more spiritual areas. He is moving out from under doctrinal authority into direct personal, spiritual experience and coming under the direct authority which contact with Christ and His disciples, the Masters, gives.[13]—Alice A. Bailey

Now, an international grass-roots movement—made up of people from all religions and no religions—is gathering in spirit to forge an experience of universal oneness. This experience —unorganized, spontaneous, international, and inspired—will ultimately join all hearts.[14] —Marianne Williamson

On the Day of Declaration, I submit, everyone—even the fundamentalists—will know, through the overshadowing of the minds of all humanity—a Pentecostal experience for all— that Maitreya is the Christ.[15] —Benjamin Creme

In the twinkling of an eye, we are all changed by this experi-ence. It is a mass *metanoia*, a shared spiritual experience for the human race, a peaceful sec-ond coming of the divine in us *as* us.[16]—Barbara Marx Hubbard

---

EXPERIENCE VS. THE WORD CONTINUED

DIRECT QUOTES FROM THE NEW AGE "GOD" AND "CHRIST"

A universal theology is impossible, but a universal experience is not only possible but necessary. ("Jesus," *ACIM Manual*, p. 77)

Truth can only be experienced. It cannot be described and it cannot be explained. ("Jesus," *ACIM Text*, p. 150)

Words will mean little now. We use them but as guides on which we do not now depend. For now we seek direct experience of truth alone. ("Jesus," *ACIM Workbook*, p. 398)

Listen to your *feelings*. Listen to your Highest Thoughts. Listen to your experience. Whenever any one of these differ from what you've been told by your teachers, or read in your books, forget the words. *Words are the least reliable purveyor of Truth.* (Walsch's "God," *CWG Book 1*, p. 8)

I am leading you to a new kind of experience that you will become less and less willing to deny. ("Jesus," *ACIM Text*, p. 207)

I do not want you to believe in me, or not to believe in me, I want you to experience me. (Maitreya, *MM: Vol. 2*, p. 10)

This wedding takes place between me—Christ—and all humans who are willing it with their whole being now. Through this marriage you experience the ecstasy of union with me. (Hubbard's "Christ," *Revelation*, pp. 294-295).

The Master is within you. If you follow the disciplines of life the Teacher teaches you, the Master reveals himself within you. Do not be attached to the human form. The living truth is a matter of experience. (Maitreya, *ETEB*, p. 56)

[Pages 122-124 excerpted from: *A Course in Miracles*; *Conversations with God: Books 1 & 3* and *Friendship with God* by N.D. Walsch; *Extraordinary Times, Extraordinary Beings* by W.S. Peterson; *Messages from Maitreya*; *Maitreya's Mission: Volume Two* by B. Creme; and *The Revelation* by B.M. Hubbard.]

CHAPTER ELEVEN

THE FINAL WORD

> ...and if in the land of peace, wherein thou
> trustedest, they wearied thee, then how wilt
> thou do in the swelling of Jordan?
> —Jeremiah 12:5

WHILE visiting a country store, I discovered a small yellow book almost hidden on a back shelf. It was titled *The Worst-Case Scenario Survival Handbook*. I picked up a copy and glanced through the book. Throughout the guide, the importance of "expecting the unexpected" and of "being prepared" were continually emphasized. Every other page seemed to teach the reader how to survive some new kind of highly precarious, worst-case scenario. How to escape from killer bees. How to survive a poisonous snake attack. How to survive an earthquake. How to escape from a mountain lion. How to survive if your parachute fails to open. The list went on and on. Under the Boy Scout motto of "Be prepared," I read the first sentence of the authors' preface:

> The principle behind this book is a simple one: You just never know.[1]

I continued reading.

> You never really know what curves life will throw at you, what is lurking around the corner, what is

hovering above, what is swimming beneath the surface. You never know when you might be called upon to perform an act of extreme bravery and to choose life or death with your own actions.[2]

As I stood there reading, I thought of September 11th. These tragic events had revealed just how unprepared we were as a nation for the worst-case type scenarios that suddenly exploded in New York City, Washington, D.C., and the Pennsylvania countryside. It was reported that those whose job it was to foresee such things grossly underestimated our adversaries. They had never even considered, much less prepared for, those kinds of situations. We had been caught unawares.

But now, in the aftermath of the disasters, we are more vigilant. We are not minimizing or denying the potential for danger. We are anticipating our adversaries as never before. And we are preparing in advance for these kinds of worst-case scenarios.

But what about the Church? Have we learned anything from September 11th? While Church "leaders" talk of "blessings" and "revival," is Jesus Christ the only one warning us to "watch and pray" and "be not deceived"? Is Jesus the only one warning us that our spiritual adversaries want to steal our faith and forever silence our testimony? Is Jesus the only one who is warning us to beware of insidious spiritual schemes like the Armageddon alternative that offers "world peace" in exchange for your soul? Is Jesus the only one willing to warn us about things like the "selection process" and that we may have to die for what we believe—that we had better be open to the possibility that our worst-case scenario may already be on its way?

These things have I spoken unto you, that ye should not be offended. They shall put you out of the synagogues: yea, the time cometh, that whosoever killeth you will think that he doeth God service. And these things will they do unto you, because they have not known the Father, nor me. But these things have I told you, that when the time shall come, ye may remember that I told you of them. (John 16:1-4)

How fortunate we are to have a Saviour who doesn't just tell us what we want to hear, but tells us what we *need* to hear, and *must* hear, so that we will be prepared for any persecution that might come our way. Especially so that we will not be caught unawares by any of our adversary's schemes and devices.

As I finished looking through *The Worst-Case Scenario Survival Handbook*, I thought of the New Age/New Gospel and of all the people who will one day be deceived into thinking that the Antichrist is Christ. If I were the author, I would add one more scenario to my practical book: "How to discern the difference between the coming of Jesus Christ and the coming of Antichrist." I would warn of the dangers of the New Gospel and its false New Age "Christ." Why? Because "you just never know."

As I walked out of the country store, I was so grateful that God has provided us with everything we need to know about salvation, truth, and deception. And that while He tells us of his blessings and eternal love, He also prepares us for the time of the end. That, lo He is with us, even through things like the "selection process," and even unto the end of time (Matthew 28:20).

Jesus Tells it Like it Is

JESUS Christ tells it like it is. He warns that danger and death and spiritual deception will characterize the time of the end. And at that time a spiritual imposter will come and convince the world that he is Christ. What will look like a great "move of God" will not be a move of God at all. Jesus tells us in Matthew 24:24 that "great signs and wonders" will accompany this deceiver—and the world will be conquered supernaturally by seemingly "wonderful" schemes and devices (2 Thessalonians 2:9-11; Daniel 8:24). Jesus warns that this false "Christ" will be so deceptive that, if it were possible, even the elect will be deceived (Mark 13:22).

Thirty years ago I was very involved with *A Course in Miracles* and New Age/New Gospel teachings. I wanted peace in my life, and I wanted to help bring peace to the world. I truly thought I had found the way to do it. Without the Lord's intervention, I would probably still be following those teachings. And if that were the case, I would most likely be applauding Marianne Williamson and The Global Renaissance Alliance/Peace Alliance instead of now warning people about them. I was sincere, but I was sincerely wrong. And so are they. The New Age/New Gospel/New Spirituality is *not* from God.

The amazing thing is that two thousand years ago Jesus Christ warned us about everything that is going on today. He told us this was going to happen and that we had better be ready. But the Church today is not ready. Ignorant of our adversary's schemes, we are missing our opportunities to expose these false teachings to a lost and dying world. Ignorant of our adversary's schemes, we don't contend for our faith because we don't seem to realize that someone is trying to steal our faith away from us. Ignorant of our adversary's schemes, we have become vulnerable to those schemes. People calling themselves Christians expecting only revival and a Kingdom of God on earth may be shocked to suddenly find themselves in the middle of great delusion, facing Antichrist instead.

I have tried as best I could to present an overview of the accelerated spiritual deception that has moved into the world over the last several decades: how the spirit world's deception has been purposeful, consistent, and highly coordinated in the ways it has presented its New Age Gospel teachings and its false New Age Christ—how these teachings have deceived many well-intentioned people into following and furthering its cause—how this deception fulfills the prophetic warnings contained in Scripture—how The Global Renaissance Alliance/Peace Alliance is a sign of the times as New Age/New Gospel/New Spirituality advocates begin to present a more united spiritual and political front—and how key members of this organization are now being called upon by the media, in the midst of crisis, to provide spiritual answers to a vulnerable nation.

I have also tried to demonstrate how hostile this false Christ is toward the real Jesus Christ and toward all believers. It must be remembered that were this false Christ to soon appear on earth, his counterfeiting of the true Christ's coming would necessarily include counterfeiting the judgment that the Bible describes as coming with Jesus Christ (Jude 14-15; 2 Thessalonians 1:8-9). Citing Scripture, the false Christ could immediately pronounce judgment on all those who "choose" to be "separate" and refuse to affirm or "experience" themselves as "a part of God." In "the twinkling of an eye," as the rest of the world is being demonically "changed" and "glorified," resisters may have to face something like the "selection process."

As someone who came out of New Age teachings, I have been deeply saddened by the Church's apathy about what is going on. Christian "leadership" has largely ignored and discounted the prophetic significance of the New Age/New Spirituality deception that is so prevalent all around us. To speak only of "revival," "blessings," and "breakthroughs" will not prepare believers for the persecution and tribulation that may soon take place.

Jesus was honest and straightforward with everyone. He did not try to please them. He said if the world called Him "Beelzebub" or "Satan," it would call His followers "Beelzebub" and "Satan," too (Matthew 10:25). He said that because the world hated and persecuted Him, it would hate and persecute His followers, also. And He said that following Him—particularly in the end days—could very well mean the loss of your life.

Jesus simply told it like it was. And He was not at all amused when followers like Peter tried to minimize, discount, or deny the things He was telling them. The Bible records in Matthew 16:21-23 that Jesus told His disciples that the world was about to kill Him, but that He would be raised again on the third day. Peter, refusing to believe the Lord's words, "rebuked" Him and insisted instead that what Jesus was telling them would not come to pass:

Be it far from thee, Lord: this shall not be unto thee.

Completely unmoved by Peter's attempt to put a "positive spin" on things, Jesus addressed the spirit that was motivating Peter's denial:

> Get thee behind me, Satan: thou art an offense unto me: for thou savourest not the things that be of God, but those that be of men.

And the Lord is saying the same thing now to those in the Church who refuse to see what is going on in the world today. God is not in the process of giving the Church "new revelation" that will supersede what He has already given us in His Holy Word. He is not in the process of bringing a "new thing" into the Church. He is not in the process of taking His Church to a "new place" or to a "new dimension" or to a "new level." He is not in the process of bringing in a "new dispensation." And He most certainly is not in the process of introducing a new gospel that contradicts in word and spirit everything He has ever taught us about our life in Jesus Christ. No, these are the plans of Antichrist, and the Church had better beware.

God's message today is loud and clear. This is not a time for celebration. This is not a time for the Church to be expecting some kind of a special blessing. This is a time to be sober and vigilant. This is a time to watch and pray. This is a time to be spiritually prepared. This is a time to be warning your brothers and sisters and family and friends about what is happening in the world.

> Be sober, be vigilant; because your adversary the devil, as a roaring lion, walketh about, seeking whom he may devour: Whom resist stedfast in the faith, knowing that the same afflictions are accomplished in your brethren that are in the world. (1 Peter 5:8-9)

When storms with the potential to kill are just offshore, reasonable people make reasonable preparations. They don't party in the face of the impending danger. They don't sit on their front porches pretending that nothing is happening. Jesus warned in Scripture that storms would come. He particularly warned about those that would come at the end of time. He wasn't being negative. He wasn't trying to scare us. He was telling us these things ahead of time so that we would be prepared; so that we would not be deceived nor intimidated nor frightened into compromising or questioning our faith. Jesus said that if we listened to His words and applied them to our lives, that our faith would withstand any storm.

> Therefore whosoever heareth these sayings of mine, and doeth them, I will liken him unto a wise man, which built his house upon a rock: And the rain descended, and the floods came, and the winds blew, and beat upon that house; and it fell not: for it was founded upon a rock. (Matthew 7:24-25)

Jesus' warnings in Matthew 24 and in the Bible's Book of Revelation are echoed throughout the Bible. God warns of a great deception at the end of time and He tells us to "be not deceived." He tells us these things in advance so that whether it is the New Age "selection process" with its "shock of a fire," or something else, we will not be surprised or think it strange.

> Beloved, think it not strange concerning the fiery trial which is to try you, as though some strange thing happened unto you: But rejoice, inasmuch as ye are partakers of Christ's sufferings; that, when his glory shall be revealed, ye may be glad also with exceeding joy. (1 Peter 4:12)

After Jesus rebuked Peter for not believing what He was telling them about His own death, He reminded His disciples that in following Him they would be subject to the same forces and the same kind of death. Following Him was a serious matter and counting the cost was part of the faith.

> Then said Jesus unto his disciples, If any man will come after me, let him deny himself, and take up his cross, and follow me. For whosoever will save his life shall lose

it: and whosoever will lose his life for my sake shall find it. For what is a man profited, if he shall gain the whole world, and lose his own soul? or what shall a man give in exchange for his soul? (Matthew 16:24-26)

There is a new world order and a new world religion coming with a false "Christ" at its head. Characterized by mass "enlightenment" and under the spell of this false "Christ," humanity will be under the great "delusion" that it is divine. While the Bible describes this New Age as a period of ultimate deception, the world will see it as a time of peace and safety, and a spiritual renaissance of the highest order. But they will be deeply deceived.

May we all pray for the truth in our heart of hearts and ask the Spirit of the Lord to lead us through these difficult and turbulent times. May we not be deceived by a spirit and a "Force" that is not from God. And may we be given the strength to endure whatever may befall us in the coming days, in Jesus' name. Amen.

> But ye, brethren, are not in darkness, that that day should overtake you as a thief. Ye are all the children of light, and the children of the day: we are not of the night, nor of darkness. Therefore let us not sleep, as do others; but let us watch and be sober.
> —1 Thessalonians 5:4–6

APPENDICES

The coming of Christ and the coming of the antichrist

According to Scripture

Key to discerning the true Christ: The true Christ, Jesus Christ, first meets His followers "in the air," *not* on the earth (1 Thessalonians 4:17). What's more, when He returns to the earth, He will return in the clouds, and everyone on earth will see him as his appearance will fill the heavens and will light up the sky (Revelation 1:7; Matthew 24:27).

Key to discerning Antichrist: Antichrist (or any false Christ) meets his followers on the earth and not in the air. **Test:** If you are standing on this earth and a "Christ" figure is also standing on this earth, and you have not previously and literally met this "Christ" figure "in the air," then that "Christ" figure is a false Christ. **Test:** Any "Christ" figure who does not teach that Jesus Christ is the one and only true Christ and that he came in the flesh to this earth, fails the Bible's test of the spirits (1 John 4:1-3).

The coming of the true Christ

Acts 1:11 [T]his same Jesus, which is taken up from you into heaven, shall so come in like manner as ye have seen him go into heaven.

Revelation 1:7 Behold, he cometh with clouds; and every eye shall see him, and they also which pierced him: and all kindreds of the earth shall wail because of him. Even so, Amen.

Mark 13:24-25 But in those days, after that tribulation, the sun shall be darkened, and the moon shall not give her light, And the stars of heaven shall fall, and the powers that are in heaven shall be shaken.

Matthew 24:27 For as the lightning cometh out of the east, and shineth even unto the west; so shall also the coming of the Son of man be.

Mark 13:26-27 And then shall they see the Son of man coming in the clouds with great power and glory. And then shall he send his angels, and shall gather together his elect from the four winds, from the uttermost part of the earth to the uttermost part of heaven.

1 Thessalonians 4:16-18 For the Lord himself shall descend from heaven with a shout, with the voice of the archangel, and with the trump of God: and the dead in Christ shall rise first: Then we which are alive and remain shall be caught up together with them in the clouds, to meet the Lord in the air: and so shall we ever be with the Lord. Wherefore comfort one another with these words.

THE COMING OF ANTICHRIST

Matthew 24:26 Wherefore if they shall say unto you, Behold, he is in the desert; go not forth: behold, he is in the secret chambers; believe it not.

Mark 13:21-23 And then if any man shall say to you, Lo, here is Christ; or, lo, he is there; believe him not: For false Christs and false prophets shall rise, and shall shew signs and wonders, to seduce, if it were possible, even the elect.

Luke 21:8 And he said, Take heed that ye be not deceived: for many shall come in my name, saying, I am Christ; and the time draweth near: go ye not therefore after them.

2 Thessalonians 2:1-4 Now we beseech you, brethren, by the coming of our Lord Jesus Christ, and by our gathering together unto him, That ye be not soon shaken in mind, or be troubled, neither by spirit, nor by word, nor by letter as from us, as that the day of Christ is at hand. Let no man deceive you by any means: for that day shall not come, except there come a falling away first, and

THE COMING OF ANTICHRIST CONTINUED

that man of sin be revealed, the son of perdition; Who opposeth and exalteth himself above all that is called God, or that is worshipped; so that he as God sitteth in the temple of God, shewing himself that he is God.

2 Thessalonians 2:9-11 Even him, whose coming is after the working of Satan with all power and signs and lying wonders, And with all deceivableness of unrighteousness in them that perish; because they received not the love of the truth, that they might be saved. And for this cause God shall send them strong delusion, that they should believe a lie.

1 John 4:1-3 Beloved, believe not every spirit, but try the spirits whether they are of God: because many false prophets are gone out into the world. Hereby know ye the Spirit of God: Every spirit that confesseth that Jesus Christ is come in the flesh is of God: And every spirit that confesseth not that Jesus Christ is come in the flesh is not of God: and this is that spirit of antichrist, whereof ye have heard that it should come; and even now already is it in the world.

Daniel 8:23-25 And in the latter time of their kingdom, when the transgressors are come to the full, a king of fierce countenance, and understanding dark sentences, shall stand up. And his power shall be mighty, but not by his own power: and he shall destroy wonderfully, and shall prosper, and practise, and shall destroy the mighty and the holy people. And through his policy also he shall cause craft to prosper in his hand; and he shall magnify himself in his heart, and by peace shall destroy many: he shall also stand up against the Prince of princes; but he shall be broken without hand.

Daniel 7:25 And he shall speak great words against the most High, and shall wear out the saints of the most High, and think to change times and laws: and they shall be given into his hand until a time and times and the dividing of time.

Daniel 11:36 [A]nd he shall exalt himself, and magnify himself above every god, and shall speak marvellous things against the God of gods, and shall prosper till the indignation be accomplished: for that that is determined shall be done.

SELECTED EXAMPLES OF FALSE TEACHINGS REGARDING JESUS' RETURN

FALSE TEACHINGS

A truth hard for the orthodox thinker of any faith to accept is the fact that *Christ cannot return because He has always been here upon our Earth*, watching over the spiritual destiny of humanity. (Bailey, *Reappearance*, p. 43)

Make known to all that I am here, that I am returned and prepare men for the Day of Declaration, the day of God's Gift. (Maitreya, *Messages*, p. 52)

The time of My Emergence has arrived; and soon, now, in full vision and fact, My face and words will become known. May you quickly recognise Me, My dear friends, My dear ones, and help your brothers to do likewise. (Maitreya, *Messages*, p. 52)

TRUE TEACHINGS

Then we which are alive and remain shall be caught up together with them in the clouds, to meet the Lord in the air: and so shall we ever be with the Lord. (1 Thessalonians 4:17)

And then if any man shall say to you, Lo, here is Christ; or, lo, he is there; believe him not: For false Christs and false prophets shall rise, and shall shew signs and wonders, to seduce, if it were possible, even the elect. But take ye heed: behold, I have foretold you all things. (Mark 13:21–23)

Which also said, Ye men of Galilee, why stand ye gazing up into heaven? this same Jesus, which is taken up from you into heaven, shall so come in like manner as ye have seen him go into heaven. (Acts 1:11)

FALSE TEACHINGS	TRUE TEACHINGS
(Q) [to Creme] Did He just sort of appear somewhere? (A) No; He came into the world by aeroplane and so fulfilled the prophecy of "coming in the clouds." On July 8th 1977 He descended from the Himalaya into the Indian subcontinent and went to one of the chief cities there. He had an acclimatisation period between July 8th and 18th, and then, on the 19th, entered a certain modern country by aeroplane. He is now an ordinary man in the world—an extraordinary, ordinary man. (Creme, *Reappearance*, p. 55)	For as the lightning cometh out of the east, and shineth even unto the west; so shall also the coming of the Son of man be. (Matthew 24:27) Behold, he cometh with clouds; and every eye shall see him, and they also which pierced him: and all kindreds of the earth shall wail because of him. Even so, Amen. (Revelation 1:7)
On July 19th 1977 He implemented the third phase—His direct physical Presence in the world. He will be seen and known by all when He reveals that Presence to the waiting world. This will take place when enough people are responding to the Teaching and energies which are emanating from His undisclosed point of focus in the modern world; and when the new direction which humanity must take has already begun to be established. Men must desire these changes for themselves; and begin implementing them of their own free will—thus showing they are ready for the new Revelation and Teaching which He brings. (Creme, *Reappearance*, p. 36)	Then if any man shall say unto you, Lo, here is Christ, or there; believe it not. For there shall arise false Christs, and false prophets, and shall shew great signs and wonders; insomuch that, if it were possible, they shall deceive the very elect. Behold, I have told you before. Wherefore if they shall say unto you, Behold, he is in the desert; go not forth: behold, he is in the secret chambers; believe it not. (Matthew 24:23-26)

FALSE TEACHINGS

When enough people are responding to His teaching He will allow Himself to be discovered. They will go back to their countries and say that the Christ is in the world, and that you should look to that country from which a certain Teaching is emanating. This will draw the attention of the media of the world to that country, and hence to Him. He will acknowledge His true Status as the Christ and will be invited to speak to the world. (Creme, *Reappearance*, p. 51)

As the Planetary Smile ripples through the nervous systems of earth and the Instant of Co-operation begins, empathy floods the feelings of the whole body of Earth, separateness is overcome, and I appear to all of you at once. I appear to you from within as a voice, and as a vision of yourself as an evolving being. I appear to you from beyond as the light being that I now am. Your electronic media will pulse with light—the same light your mystics see. (Hubbard's "Christ," *Revelation*, p. 245)

TRUE TEACHINGS

And he said, Take heed that ye be not deceived: for many shall come in my name, saying, I am Christ; and the time draweth near: go ye not therefore after them. (Luke 21:8)

And Jesus answered and said unto them, Take heed that no man deceive you. For many shall come in my name, saying, I am Christ; and shall deceive many. (Matthew 24:4-5)

Even him, whose coming is after the working of Satan with all power and signs and lying wonders, And with all deceivableness of unrighteousness in them that perish; because they received not the love of the truth, that they might be saved. And for this cause God shall send them strong delusion, that they should believe a lie. (2 Thessalonians 2:9-11)

FALSE TEACHINGS	TRUE TEACHINGS
Each shall be "sealed" with the seal of the living God. This means that they shall be marked, visibly identified, first to themselves, then to others. (Hubbard's "Christ," *Revelation*, p. 149)	And he causeth all, both small and great, rich and poor, free and bond, to receive a mark in their right hand, or in their foreheads: And that no man might buy or sell, save he that had the mark, or the name of the beast, or the number of his name. Here is wisdom. Let him that hath understanding count the number of the beast: for it is the number of a man; and his number is Six hundred threescore and six. (Revelation 13:16–18)
Those with the seal of the living God on their foreheads will be with Christ at the time of the Transformation. (p. 190)	

You are to be transported to the new Jerusalem. . . . You will be "taken up" at the appropriate time. . . . What does "taken up" mean? It is a complex transformation. You enter a state of universal consciousness. . . . In this state of God-centered bliss, you are physically awakened by an inner electricity that changes the frequency of the atoms in your body. . . . Due to the God-centered awareness and the physical transfiguration, your brain/body "ascends" to the next level of being. (Hubbard's "Christ," *Revelation*, p. 270)	For the Lord himself shall descend from heaven with a shout, with the voice of the archangel, and with the trump of God: and the dead in Christ shall rise first: Then we which are alive and remain shall be caught up together with them in the clouds, to meet the Lord in the air: and so shall we ever be with the Lord. (1 Thessalonians 4:16–17)

[Excerpted from: *Messages from Maitreya the Christ*; *The Reappearance of the Christ and the Masters of Wisdom*, B. Creme; *The Revelation*, B.M. Hubbard; *The Reappearance of Christ*, A.A. Bailey.]

A COURSE IN MIRACLES AND THE BIBLE

DIRECT QUOTES FROM THE "JESUS" OF THE COURSE	DIRECT QUOTES FROM THE BIBLE
GOD	**GOD**
There is no separation of God and His creation. (*Text*, p. 147)	Who changed the truth of God into a lie, and worshipped and served the creature more than the Creator, who is blessed for ever. (Romans 1:25)
When God created you He made you part of Him. (*Text*, p. 100)	
MAN	**MAN**
The recognition of God is the recognition of yourself. (*Text*, p. 147)	I am God, and not man; the Holy One in the midst of thee. (Hosea 11:9)
JESUS	**JESUS**
Is he [Jesus] the Christ? O yes, along with you. (*Manual*, p. 87)	Take heed that no man deceive you. For many shall come in my name, saying, I am Christ; and shall deceive many. (Matthew 24: 4–5)
NAME OF JESUS	**NAME OF JESUS**
The Name of Jesus Christ as such is but a symbol. . . . It is a symbol that is safely used as a replacement for the many names of all the gods to which you pray. (*Manual*, p. 58)	Wherefore God also hath highly exalted him, and given him a name which is above every name. (Philippians 2:9)

CROSS/CRUCIFIXION

A slain Christ has no meaning. (*Text*, p. 425)

Do not make the pathetic error of "clinging to the old rugged cross." (*Text*, p. 52)

The journey to the cross should be the last "useless journey." (*Text*, p. 52)

SIN

There is no sin; it has no consequence. (*Workbook*, p. 183)

EVIL

Innocence is wisdom because it is unaware of evil, and evil does not exist. (*Text*, p. 38)

DEVIL

The "devil" is a frightening concept because he seems to be extremely powerful and extremely active. . . . This makes absolutely no sense. (*Text*, pp. 49–50)

THE BIBLE

Words will mean little now. We use them but as guides on which we do not now depend. For now we seek direct experience of truth alone. (*Workbook*, p. 298)

CROSS/CRUCIFIXION

And that he might reconcile both unto God in one body by the cross, having slain the enmity thereby. (Ephesians 2:16)

For the preaching of the cross is to them that perish foolishness; but unto us which are saved it is the power of God. (1 Corinthians 1:18)

SIN

If we say that we have no sin, we deceive ourselves, and the truth is not in us. (1 John 1:8)

EVIL

Abhor that which is evil; cleave to that which is good. (Romans 12:9)

DEVIL

Be sober, be vigilant; because your adversary the devil, as a roaring lion, walketh about, seeking whom he may devour. (1 Peter 5:8)

THE BIBLE

All scripture is given by inspiration of God, and is profitable for doctrine, for reproof, for correction, for instruction in righteousness. (2 Timothy 3:16)

ENDNOTES

1/HELEN SCHUCMAN, MARIANNE WILLIAMSON, AND *A COURSE IN MIRACLES*

1. Robert Skutch, *Journey without Distance: The Story behind "A Course in Miracles"* (Berkeley, CA: Celestial Arts, 1984), p. 54.

2. Ibid., p. 60.

3. *A Course in Miracles: Combined Volume* (Glen Ellen, CA: Foundation for Inner Peace, 1975, 1992), (*Text*), p. 14.

4. Ibid., p. 425.

5. Marianne Williamson, *A Woman's Worth* (NY: Ballantine, 1993), p. 124.

2/BARBARA MARX HUBBARD AND *THE REVELATION*

1. Barbara Marx Hubbard, *The Revelation: A Message of Hope for the New Millennium* (Novato, CA: Nataraj Publishing, 1995), pp. 40-43; Hubbard, *The Hunger of Eve: One Woman's Odyssey Toward the Future* (Eastsound, WA: Island Pacific NW, 1989), pp. 66-68.

2. Hubbard, *The Revelation*, op. cit., p. 42.

3. Ibid., p. 55.

4. Ibid., p. 59.

5. Ibid., p. 64.

6. Barbara Marx Hubbard, *Conscious Evolution: Awakening the Power of Our Social Potential* (Novato, CA: New World Library, 1998), p. 279.

7. Hubbard, *The Hunger of Eve*, op. cit., p. 150.

8. Ibid., p. 196.

9. Hubbard, *Conscious Evolution*, op. cit., p. 116.

10. Hubbard, *The Revelation*, op. cit., pp. 67–69.

11. Ibid., p. 350.

12. Ibid., pp. 264–265.

13. Ibid., p. 298.

14. Ibid., p. 157.

15. Ibid., pp. 243–245.

16. Ibid., pp. 44 and 78–79.

17. Ibid., p. 258.

18. Ibid., pp. 240 and 267.

19. Ibid., p. 255.

20. Marianne Williamson, ed., *Imagine: What America Could Be in the 21st Century* (U.S.A.: Rodale, Inc., 2000), pp. 381–391.

21. Barbara Marx Hubbard, *Emergence: The Shift from Ego to Essence* (Charlottesville, VA: Hampton Roads, 2001), pp. 118–121.

3/NEALE DONALD WALSCH AND *CONVERSATIONS WITH GOD*

1. Neale Donald Walsch, *Conversations with God: an uncommon dialogue, Book 1* (NY: G.P. Putnam's Sons, Hardcover Edition 1996), p. 1.

2. Ibid., p. 2.

3. Ibid., p. 95.

4. Ibid., p. 192.

5. Neale Donald Walsch, *Conversations with God: an uncommon dialogue, Book 2* (Charlottesville, VA: Hampton Roads, 1997), p. 35.

6. Ibid., p. 56.

7. Ibid., p. 36.

8. Neale Donald Walsch, *Questions and Answers on "Conversations with God"* (Charlottesville, VA: Hampton Roads, 1999), p. 334.

9. The Global Renaissance Alliance (http://web.archive.org/web/20060115103911/http://www.renaissancealliance.org/resrce/board.htm).

10. Neale Donald Walsch, *Conversations with God: an uncommon dialogue, Book 3* (Charlottesville, VA: Hampton Roads, 1998), p. 256.

11. Walsch, *Conversations with God: Book 1*, op. cit., p. 41.

12. Ibid., p. 76.

13. Walsch, *Conversations with God: Book 2*, op. cit., p. 235.

14. Ibid., p. 126.

15. Walsch, *Conversations with God: Book 3*, op. cit., p. 320.

16. Walsch, *Conversations with God: Book 1*, op. cit., p. 90.

17. Neale Donald Walsch, *Friendship with God* (New York, NY: G.P. Putnam's Sons, 1999), pp. 295-296.

18. Ibid., p. 394.

19. Ibid., p. 376.

20. Walsch, *Conversations with God: Book 2*, op. cit., p. 141.

21. Walsch, *Friendship with God*, op. cit., p. 375.

4/BENJAMIN CREME, WAYNE PETERSON, AND MAITREYA

1. Wayne S. Peterson, *Extraordinary Times, Extraordinary Beings: Experiences of an American Diplomat with Maitreya and the Masters of Wisdom* (Charlottesville, VA: Hampton Roads, 2001, 2003), p. ix.

2. Ibid., p. 31.

3. Ibid., p. 3.

4. Ibid., pp. 33-34.

5. Benjamin Creme, *The Reappearance of the Christ and the Masters of Wisdom* (North Hollywood, CA: The Tara Press, 1980), p. 30.

6. Peterson, *Extraordinary Times, Extraordinary Beings*, op. cit., p. 36.

7. Ibid., p. 55.

8. Ibid., p. 50.

9. Ibid., pp. ix-x.

10. Ibid., p. 100.

11. Wayne S. Peterson, author of *Extraordinary Times, Extraordinary Beings*, interviewed on *Bridging Heaven & Earth*, a weekly talk show broadcast on Cox Communications' public access Channel 17 in Santa Barbara, California on November 9, 2001 (http://www.HeaventoEarth.com).

12. Peterson, *Extraordinary Times, Extraordinary Beings*, op. cit., pp. 7-8.

13. Ibid., p. 126.

14. Ibid., p. 129.

15. Ibid., pp. 144-145.

5/THE LIGHT THAT WAS DARK

1. Warren B. Smith, *The Light That Was Dark: From the New Age to Amazing Grace* (Magalia, CA: Mountain Stream Press, 2005), pp. 145-147.
2. Ibid., pp. 151-155.
3. Ibid., pp. 155-156.

6/THE GLOBAL RENAISSANCE ALLIANCE/PEACE ALLIANCE

1. Williamson, *Imagine: What America Could Be in the 21st Century,* op. cit., p. 413.
2. Marianne Williamson, *Healing the Soul of America: Reclaiming Our Voices as Spiritual Citizens* (NY: Simon & Schuster, 1997, 2000), p. 195.

7/THE NEW AGE CAMPAIGN FOR PEACE

1. Hubbard, *The Revelation*, op. cit., p. 74.
2. *Larry King Live*, Marianne Williamson as guest, October 14, 2001, transcript from Web site (http://www.cnn.com/Transcripts/0110/14/lklw.00.html), pp. 19-20.
3. Ibid., p. 21.
4. Kenneth Wapnick, ed., *Concordance of "A Course in Miracles": A Complete Index* (NY: Penguin Books, 1997), p. 64.
5. *The Oprah Winfrey Show*, Marianne Williamson as guest, "What Really Matters Now," September 26, 2001 transcript (Livingston, NJ: Burrelle's Information Services), p. 10.
6. Ibid., p. 13.
7. Ibid., p. 14.
8. Hubbard, *The Revelation*, op. cit., p. 241.
9. *The Oprah Winfrey Show*, September 26, 2001 transcript, p. 16.
10. The Global Renaissance Alliance recommended reading list (http://web.archive.org/web/20060115103911/http://www.renaissancealliance.org/resrce/board.htm).
11. *The Oprah Winfrey Show*, Gary Zukav as guest, "Is War the Only Answer?," October 1, 2001 transcript (Livingston, NJ: Burrelle's Information Services), p. 14.
12. *The Oprah Winfrey Show*, Gary Zukav as guest, "What Do You Really Believe?," November 1, 2001 transcript (Livingston, NJ: Burrelle's Information Services) , pp. 7-8.

13. Wayne Dyer, "There's a Spiritual Solution to Every Problem," Public Broadcasting System broadcast 2001, transcribed by author. For a revealing interview with Dyer see http://www.phenomenews.com/archives/feb02/dyerw.htm.

14. Ibid.

8/THE ARMAGEDDON ALTERNATIVE

1. Wapnick, ed., *Concordance of "A Course in Miracles,"* op. cit., p. 695.

2. Hubbard, *Conscious Evolution*, op. cit., p. 43.

9/THE NEW AGE DOCTRINE OF SEPARATION

1. *Messages from Maitreya the Christ: One Hundred Forty Messages* (Los Angeles, CA: Share International Foundation, 1980), Second Edition, Second Printing 2001, p. 189.

2. Ibid., p. 248.

3. Walsch, *Friendship with God*, op. cit., p. 357.

4. Alice A. Bailey, *The Externalisation of the Hierarchy* (NY: Lucis Publishing Company: New York, 1957), Eighth Printing 1989, p. 75.

5. Walsch, *Conversations with God: Book 2*, op. cit., p. 242.

6. *A Course in Miracles: Combined Volume, (Text),* op. cit., p. 147.

7. Hubbard, *The Revelation*, op. cit., p. 233.

8. Ibid., p. 255.

9. Ibid., p. 240.

10. Ibid., p. 111.

11. This note written by Pastor Loren Decker for this book.

10/THE SILENT CHURCH

1. *NBC News Special Report: America on Alert,* Tom Brokaw hosting Marianne Williamson as guest, September 16, 2001 broadcast transcript (Livingston, NJ: Burrelle's Information Services).

2. Adolph Hitler, *Mein Kampf* (Sixth Pressing), translated by Ralph Manheim (Boston: Houghton Mifflin Co.: Mariner Books, 1999), p. *xv*.

3. Jay Gary Web site, referenced by Barbara Marx Hubbard in *Conscious Evolution*, p. 263.

4. Hubbard, *Conscious Evolution*, op. cit., p. 279.

5. Barbara Marx Hubbard and Jay Gary: originally cited at (http://www.wnrf.org/programs/awards.htm and http://www.wnrf.org/networks/christian.htm).

6. Walsch, *Conversations with God: Book 3*, op. cit., p. 325.

7. *A Course in Miracles: Combined Volume*, (*Text*), op. cit., p. 479.

8. Williamson, *Healing the Soul of America*, op. cit., p. 13.

9. Hubbard, *The Revelation*, op. cit., pp. 242–245.

10. (http://www.share-international.org/background/FAQ/faq_main.htm), *50 Frequently asked questions*: Question 16.

11. *A Course in Miracles: Combined Volume*, (*Manual for Teachers*), op. cit., p. 37.

12. Smith, *The Light That Was Dark*, op. cit., pp. 160–161.

13. Bailey, *The Externalisation of the Hierarchy*, op. cit., p. 417.

14. Williamson, *Healing the Soul of America*, op. cit., p. 205.

15. (http://www.share-international.org/background/FAQ/faq_main.htm), *50 Frequently asked questions*: Question 16.

16. Hubbard, *The Revelation*, op. cit., p. 324.

11/THE FINAL WORD

1. Joshua Piven and David Borgenicht, *The Worst-Case Scenario Survival Handbook* (San Francisco, CA: Chronicle Books, 1999), p. 14.

2. Ibid.

INDEX

R

S

BIBLIOGRAPHY

A *Course in Miracles: Combined Volume*. Glen Ellen, Calif.: Foundation for Inner Peace, 1975, 1992.

Bailey, Alice A. *The Destiny of the Nations*. New York: Lucis Publishing Company, 1949, Ninth Printing 2007.

Bailey, Alice A. *The Externalisation of the Hierarchy*. New York: Lucis Publishing Company, 1957, Eighth Printing 1989.

Bailey, Alice A. *From Bethlehem to Calvary*. New York: Lucis Publishing Company, 1937, Ninth Printing 1999.

Bailey, Alice A. *The Rays and the Initiations*. New York: Lucis Publishing Company, 1960, Tenth Printing 2002.

Bailey, Alice A. *The Reappearance of the Christ*. New York. Lucis Publishing Company, 1948, Eleventh Printing 1996.

Creme, Benjamin. *Maitreya's Mission: Volume Two*. Los Angeles: Share International Foundation, 1993, Third Printing 2004.

Creme, Benjamin. *The Reappearance of the Christ and the Masters of Wisdom*. North Hollywood: The Tara Press, 1980.

Hitler, Adolph. *Mein Kampf* (Sixth Pressing). Boston: Houghton Mifflin Company: Mariner Books, 1999.

Hubbard, Barbara Marx. *Conscious Evolution: Awakening the Power of Our Social Potential*. Novato, Calif.: New World Library, 1998.

Hubbard, Barbara Marx. *Emergence: The Shift from Ego to Essence.* Charlottsville, Virginia: Hampton Roads, 2001.

Hubbard, Barbara Marx. *The Hunger of Eve: One Woman's Odyssey Toward the Future.* Eastsound, Wash.: Island Pacific NW, 1989.

Hubbard, Barbara Marx. *The Revelation: A Message of Hope for the New Millennium.* Novato, Calif.: Nataraj Publishing, 1995.

Messages from Maitreya the Christ: One Hundred Forty Messages. Los Angeles: Share International Foundation, 1980, Second Edition, Second Printing 2001.

Peterson, Wayne S. *Extraordinary Times, Extraordinary Beings: Experiences of an American Diplomat with Maitreya and the Masters of Wisdom.* Charlottsville, Va.: Hampton Roads, 2001, 2003.

Piven, Joshua and David Borgenicht. *The Worst-Case Scenario Survival Handbook.* San Francisco: Chronicle Books, 1999.

Skutch, Robert. *Journey without Distance: The Story behind "A Course in Miracles".* Berkeley, Calif.: Celestial Arts, 1984.

Smith, Warren. *The Light That Was Dark: From the New Age to Amazing Grace.* Magalia, Calif.: Mountain Stream Press, 2005.

Walsch, Neale Donald. *Conversations with God: an uncommon dialogue, Book 1.* New York: G.P. Putnam's Sons, Hardcover Edition 1996.

Walsch, Neale Donald. *Conversations with God: an uncommon dialogue, Book 2.* Charlottsville, Va.: Hampton Roads, 1997.

Walsch, Neale Donald. *Conversations with God: an uncommon dialogue, Book 3.* Charlottsville, Va.: Hampton Roads, 1998.

Walsch, Neale Donald. *Friendship with God: an uncommon dialogue.* New York: G.P. Putnam's Sons, 1999.

Walsch, Neale Donald. *Questions and Answers on "Conversations with God".* Charlottsville, Va.: Hampton Roads, 1999.

Wapnick, Kenneth, ed. *Concordance of "A Course in Miracles"*. New York: Penguin Books, 1997.

Williamson, Marianne. *A Return to Love, Reflections on the Principles of "A Course in Miracles"*. New York: Harper Perennial, 1996.

Williamson, Marianne. *A Woman's Worth*. New York: Ballantine Books, 1993.

Williamson, Marianne. *Healing the Soul of America: Reclaiming Our Voices as Spiritual Citizens*. New York: Simon & Schuster, 1997, 2000.

Williamson, Marianne, ed. *Imagine What America Could Be in the 21st Century*. U.S.A.: Rodale Inc., 2000.

ALSO BY WARREN B. SMITH

Deceived On Purpose: The New Age Implications of the Purpose Driven Church Warns about the serious New Age implications of Rick Warren's book *The Purpose Driven Life.* Smith takes the reader into the inner workings of today's evangelical world as he explores the questionable interconnections of several of its top leaders. 212 pages, 2nd edition. $14.95. Softbound. Contact BookMasters: (800)247-6553.

The Light That Was Dark: From the New Age to Amazing Grace The personal account of how Warren B. Smith, who as a spiritual seeker, was led into the metaphysical New Age where the Christ proclaimed wasn't the real Christ at all. Concerned that today's church is being seduced by the same false teachings and the same false Christ that drew him into the New Age, Smith shares his story in a most compelling way. 168 pages, 2nd edition. $14.95. Softbound. Contact BookMasters: (800)247-6553.

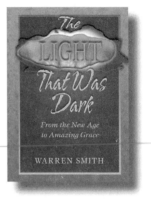

A "Wonderful" Deception: The Further New Age Implications of the Purpose Driven Movement Five years after writing *Deceived On Purpose* Warren Smith continues to reveal how Christian leaders wittingly or unwittingly are leading the church into a spiritual trap. A *"Wonderful" Deception* examines church metaphors, concepts, and beliefs that are essentially the same as those being used in today's New Age/New Spirituality teachings. 242 Pages. $14.95. Softbound. Contact Lighthouse Trails: (866)876-3910.

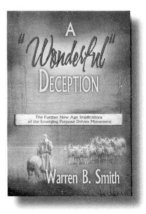